Dedicated to the people who taught me everything: Mystery, Style, Tyler, and all of the girls I've dated. Thanks to Hayden for forcing me to talk to a girl in a bar for the first time.

And to all the girls who rejected me along the way.

MAKE HER CHASE YOU

MAKE HER CHASE YOU

THE PRACTICAL GUIDE TO ATTRACTING
GIRLS WHO ARE "OUT OF YOUR LEAGUE"
EVEN IF YOU'RE NOT RICH OR HANDSOME.

For information, e-mail tynan@tynan.net.

Cover graphic licensed from Andrejs Zavadskis.

Hmm. Not much else to write on this page.

ISBN 1-440-46154-6

Introduction

I'm proud of my involvement in the pickup community, both as a student and as a teacher who is able to help others reach their goals.

This pride has led me to explain pickup to countless people that I've met throughout the years. Most are intrigued by the idea and eager to learn more, but some declare that it's immoral and refuse to even consider reading about it.

I'm of the opinion that pickup is not just a moral, but also a noble pursuit.

My years spent learning pickup, and thus learning to be a more attractive person, are my gift to women that I am involved with presently and will be involved with in the future. They have the benefit of being with a guy who has weeded out all of his unattractive characteristics and truly understands how they think and feel.

Learning pickup is something you should be proud of. You've taken a step that many men should take, but few actually muster the courage necessary.

I was embarrassed at first, but by the time I got good and was actually having success with women, I was so proud that I would tell each of the girls I met about it with enthusiasm. Every single one was fascinated, more attracted to me, and curious to learn more.

One night Style and I were at a birthday party, bouncing around talking to different groups of people.

We found two attractive girls named Karen and Jennifer. Within a few minutes, Style was talking with Jennifer and I had sat down with Karen. She was a smart girl who was a competitive runner. We liked each other, and exchanged numbers.

When she called (yes, girls will be calling you first too) I told her to first meet at my place, as I had something to show her.

What I didn't tell her is that I was in the middle of teaching a workshop with Mystery in our living room.

She got there, sat with me, and listened as I taught students how to tell stories. As we were about to leave to get some ice cream, a student asked how to stop a girl walking on the street. Using Karen, I showed him. She enjoyed being part of the demonstration. We said our goodbyes and headed for the door.

"Herbal, I have one last question. When a girl's in your bed and won't sleep with you, what do you do?"

I laughed and answered him. Karen was amused too, not mortified as some may expect. The simple truth is that both guys and girls are looking for intimate relationships, connection, and attraction. Anything a member of either gender can do to get closer to those goals is ethical and downright generous.

Or, to put it another way—if a girl was trying hard to become more attractive to you, how upset would you be about it?

Who am I?

My real name is Tynan, but I'm better known as "Herbal", thanks to the now infamous book by Neil Strauss, *The Game*.

Except for a short stint in third grade, I was never popular. I always had great friends, but almost all of them were male.

I was too shy to talk to girls. Way too shy.

I had one girlfriend in High School, and it would be fair to say that she picked me up.

Near the end of high school, a beautiful girl named Julie fell for me. She was a friend of a friend and by rare coincidence happened to spend enough time around me to like me.

I, of course, liked her as well. Because I was unable to interact with girls, we remained "just friends". Being as shy and passive as I was, I accepted this.

Then, during the last week of summer, something changed.

One lazy summer night we went to a party together that her girlfriends hosted. My shyness rearing its ugly head again, I didn't talk to anyone. I just followed her around.

She got a phone call and I followed her into the bathroom while she answered it. After she hung up, she looked at me, pasued, and said, "Tynan, I have something to confess to you. You're going to be mad at me."

"Okay?"

I had no idea what to think.

"I … I have a crush on you," she said coyly, her gaze dropping to the floor.

I felt that adrenaline rush that only girls can trigger and replied, "I have a crush on you too." We kissed for the first time, and it was one of few kisses in my life that I'll always remember.

Unfortunately for our belated summer romance, she was leaving to go to school in Chicago in just three days.

When she left, it was over. I naively assumed that we would have a long distance relationship, but she had more sense than that.

I was in love, and I missed her. My pillow still smelled like her perfume, and I would smell it every night before I went to sleep, until one day I couldn't smell it anymore.

To use the parlance of the pickup community, I was an AFC – an average frustrated chump.

Over the next year I built a business. If I was rich, maybe she would want to be with me when she got back from school. I was so blind to reality that I thought that waiting four years for her was a good idea.

Whenever I worked on my business, I thought of her and let that thought motivate me.

I began training to run. I pushed myself until I could run ten miles, thinking that maybe if I was in better shape, I might have a chance with her. As I battled across the pavement I thought of her, and that thought kept me motivated.

One day a friend showed me a web site that claimed to teach guys how to meet women. I thought it was a stupid idea, and I continued with my futile effort to make myself better for Julie.

Three years passed, and I had only one girlfriend during that time. It lasted six months, and although she initiated much of it, I learned that I was very good at keeping girls once I had them. It was a relief to know that at least I had some natural skill with women.

During those three years, Julie got engaged and decided to stay in Chicago. Things were looking bleak.

Finally one night I lay down in bed and thought of Julie, as I often did. But this time, I was angry at myself. I deserved better than to pine over one girl I had no chance with. I got up and turned on my computer.

I began trying to find that site again. I couldn't remember what it was called. I punched different permutations of "seduction" "pickup" "fast" and "quick" until I finally found it. The site was *www.fastseduction.com*.

I spent the entire night reading the site, not going to bed until the sun made it nearly impossible.

When I woke up late in the afternoon, eight hours later, I picked up reading where I left off.

Over the next few months I read everything there was to know about pickup, but was still too shy to practice it. Eventually newfound pickup friends pushed me into it, and I started talking to girls. I had very moderate success.

I decided that if I was going to do this, I needed to immerse myself and dedicate myself to it. Before I could do that, I wanted to see the greats in person to see what was possible. Knowing that there was a *Double your Dating* seminar there, I booked a ticket to Chicago.

The seminar was sold out, but I didn't care. All I needed was a tiny peek into the world of the pickup artists.

Tyler from Real Social Dynamics was, and still is, one of the greatest pickup artists in the world. Through a fortunate set of coincidences, he allowed me to observe his workshop for free, and I saw Tyler in action.

He stole Miss Indiana from her boyfriend, all no further than five feet in front of me.

His business partner, Papa, was spearheading an endeavor called "Project Hollywood" where the best pickup artists in the world would live together in a mansion right in the middle of the Hollywood clubbing district. Mystery, Style, Tyler, and Papa were all going to live there.

I became friends with Papa, and he invited me to join Mystery's Lounge, which was a secret forum that only the top pickup artists in the world had access to.

He must have thought I was a lot better pickup artist than I was, because I had no business being there.

A week after I joined the lounge, I saw a post from Style saying that they had one bedroom in Project Hollywood left. Rent was $3000 per month, but I that barely phased me. It was a once in a lifetime opportunity to learn from the most skilled ladies men in the land.

Before I could second guess myself, I called Style and agreed to take the room. I knew that if I didn't, I would always wonder what could have happened.

Three weeks later I had told all my friends and family about my involvement with pickup and was on the road to Los Angeles. Fueled by adrenaline and visions in my head of adventures to come, I drove there in 24 hours without stopping to sleep.

On the road there I had a scary thought for the first time - was I going to be part of their project, or just a tenant? I had only met Papa and Tyler, and didn't really know them well. How much would they actually be willing to teach me?

I got my answer the first night when Mystery took me out as his wingman. I soon became close friends with everyone in the house, and each one actively contributed towards me becoming a better pickup artist. I attended their seminars, went out with them, and asked them countless questions. We winged together, compared notes, and went on double dates together.

Long nights were spent in the hot tub discussing pickup and life's possibilities.

The pickup education I received was second to none. I learned from everyone who was anyone in the pickup scene, and went out with them to do my homework in Hollywood's hottest clubs.

I was quickly transformed from an introverted computer nerd to a bona fide pickup artist.

Eventually it began to rain in paradise. Mystery and Papa fought and refused to work together. I watched my roommates turn from friends to enemies.

Taking Papa's place, I began managing Mystery's workshops initially, and later would travel around the US to help teach them with him. As I taught workshops with Mystery I earned his respect as a pickup artist, and my skills grew.

Things were going swimmingly until I stole his girlfriend, Katya.

If you've read *The Game*, then you know that story.

Why my advice?

These days, much to my chagrin, there are hundreds of new so called pickup experts.

I've met a number of these people, and am consistently left unimpressed.

The truth is that there are few truly great pickup artists, and I'm happy to count all of them as my friends. In a tier of their own are Mystery, Style, Tyler, Jlaix, and Lance Mason.

These are the true masters of pickup who have innovated and shaped the way we think about the skill. I was fortunate to learn tremendous amounts from each of these people, as well as many other skilled pickup artists.

I came into the game with no ego, and happily learned from each guru when other students would latch onto only one person with fanatic loyalty, and ignore valuable teachings from others.

Many of the gurus are enemies now, and are increasingly inaccessible. I lived with some of them and learned every nuance of their philosophy and methods. In short, I've been fortunate enough to receive an education in pickup that can probably never be reproduced.

When I was in Hollywood I went out constantly with experts in the field and gained my own insight which I combined with what I'd learned. I put in the time and speak from experience.

My goal with this book is to transfer my knowledge and understanding to you as efficiently and completely as possible. You will still have to practice to become proficient, but my hope is that this book will make that journey easier, faster, and more enjoyable that would otherwise be possible.

Girls like you

Whether you actually believe it or not, I'd like to request that you allow one assumption in this book, one that I personally know is true.

When you were a baby, everyone liked you. You looked cute, you smiled, you made funny noises, and people put up with changing your diapers. If you were put into a playpen with a similarly cute girl when you were learning to crawl, you would probably play and laugh.

We start off likable by everyone. Then we pick up habits.

Some of the habits we pick up are good, but others are bad. You may know people who are naturally fantastic with women – they got lucky and picked up more good habits than bad.

Our society has a very strange view on dating and relationships, with an overemphasis on blending in and fabricated courting gestures (do sea otters trade semi-rare stones?). It's not crazy to expect that most people would have some issues with the natural and necessary process of mating.

Deep down inside, you are someone that girls like.

Unfortunately, you have learned some ridiculous habits which are preventing them from realizing that they like you. When you finally learn this, it's as if you just noticed you had red slippers. It was a long journey, and all you had to do was click your heels the whole time.

All I want to do for you is to remove your bad habits, and teach you some new good habits.

I don't want to turn you into a rock star wannabe who hangs out at clubs and calls girls "broads", unless that's who you really are. I want to amplify who you already are, and who your friends love you for being. Let's turn up the volume on all of the things that are great about you, and mute those which are distracting from your likable self.

If you're willing to trust me that somewhere in you is a very attractive guy, then my job excavating that person will be made a lot easier. This is the exact process that I've personally gone through, and I'm writing the book that I wish I could send to myself 10 years ago.

Pickup Artists vs. Naturals

The national pastime of America is complaining. We love to think that everyone has things easier than we do, and that we are victims. If you're one of those people, wake up!

I've heard so many pickup artists wish that they were naturals. I don't wish for a second that I was a natural. If I could give up the journey I've taken to become a pickup artist and trade it for natural skills, I wouldn't do it.

Naturals aren't very aware of what they're doing. Some have a basic understanding, but they never have the same frame of reference that someone who sucked with women has.

Worst of all, they're already successful, so they don't have much motivation to study the inner workings of interpersonal relationships.

Being bad with women is no fun, but be thankful that you've found resources that can totally change that. It will be an incredible journey that will leave you in the most enviable position of all.

What Attracts Women?

The natural progression of a pickup can be cut up into many different phases, but for practical purposes, I like to think of it as two phases.

The first phase only lasts 5–10 minutes, starting from when you first see the girl you're interested in. I call it "advertising", but most conventional pickup theories call it "attraction."

It's during this phase that you need to advertise that you're worth getting to know. This is the easiest place to lose a girl, so it's worthwhile to spend some time perfecting the art of the first five minutes.

Your main objective during the advertising phase is to advertise that you're different from most guys and that you're not creepy in any way. How you differentiate yourself isn't vitally important—you only need for her to decide that you're worth getting to know.

Because the first five minutes isn't used to show who I am, only that I'm different, I don't mind having it very scripted, and I may stretch the truth a bit.

I would never deceive a girl by saying I'm in a rock band or something, but I'll gladly use an old story and pretend it just happened yesterday, just like comedians do.

There are hundreds of good openers that have been popularized, and they all follow a similar pattern. The typical opener seeks the girl's opinion and is usually about relationships.

At the end of this book I have a small appendix of some of the most effective and underpublicized oponers that I like to use.

Don't become too preoccupied with an opener. The actual content of the opener isn't nearly as important as how you say it. If you focus exclusively on the opener like many people do, you'll never get good at anything other than opening.

The old standby of, "Hi, my name is Tynan and I just had to meet you." is extremely effective when delivered confidently.

Jlaix, one of the most skilled pickup artists, found that he could open groups just by saying "I like salad." You can use one of my openers or one of the hundreds easily available on the internet, but I'd recommend coming up with your own.

Although it doesn't actually matter in practice, budding pickup artists often worry that girls will realize that they're reciting canned lines. Inventing your own routines solves that problem.

The one caveat with so called opinion openers is that you don't want to seem like you don't know what to do. For example, "I met this girl and I think she likes me, but I don't really know where to take her," is awful. It shows that you're incompetent with women.

Similarly, don't try to show off. A line like "I'm dating three women right now and there's a fourth girl I'm interested in. Do you think that's too many?" seems fake (even if it's not) and reeks of bragging. Sticking to stories about your friends will ensure that you don't get caught in this trap.

I also like fake question openers. A fake question opener asks a question, but discards the answer quickly to tell a story.

For example, "Hey, have you guys ever been to Pitch and Putt Golf?"

I don't care whether they say yes or no. Either way I respond, "Oh really? Well I was there last week and..."

This is a reasonably good segue from not knowing someone to telling them a story.

Men talk in a linear fashion, while women tend to jump from subject to subject. If you jump around like they do it will feel strange to you but will feel totally normal to them.

The last type of notable opener is situational openers. These are very dangerous because they're the only kind of openers normal people tend to use.

Bad examples of situational openers are:

"Hey, this club is really busy tonight."

"That's a really cool purse. Where did you get it?"

"You're really pretty. Can I buy you a drink?"

All of these openers are boring, typical, and are not advertising anything good about you. Avoid them like the plague. Good situational openers are ones that there's no chance she's ever heard before.

I once saw a pair of girls waiting at a bus stop. I walked up to them and said, "Ladies... I'm very sorry, but the bus is out of service tonight. Luckily for you, my friend and I offer a piggyback service. You can buy rides for $1 a block."

They laughed as we tried to convince them that we were serious, and eventually we got on the bus with them to go to a salsa lesson.

No matter what you say, the important thing is to relate a very specific impression, one which will ensure that she wants to get to know you. Strive to seem as though you have a very interesting life full of friends and adventure, and that you're talking to her only to amuse yourself.

Make her feel as though you're excited about life, and that you could very easily walk away at a moment's notice.

Key to making it seem like you may leave any second is your body language. Lean back and speak louder, rather than leaning in. Face away from her at first with your body, only turning your head. Slowly turn towards her as your conversation continues, but only if she is also turning towards you. If she isn't, then take a step backwards as if you're about to leave.

Vary the intonation and timing of your speech. Speak quickly through boring parts and very slowly through exciting parts. Let your voice rise and fall through its range.

Think of how Ben Stein talks—that's how you don't want to be.

You should incorporate a lot of teasing into the first five minutes. Make it imminently clear that you don't put her on a pedestal. A dismissive "Oh, reeeallly?" or "Uh-huh." can work wonders.

These sorts of actions signal that you're on her level, and that you're not intimidated. This works doubly well if you're somewhat geeky like I am, and look like the type that might be intimidated by beauty.

She can't help but wonder what makes us so confident.If she's still talking to you and facing you after five minutes, you've done enough advertising. She's ready to stop bantering and get to know who you are.

One of the most common errors I've seen amongst pickup students is that they never move past the advertising phase. This is largely because when properly executed it causes girls to show how attracted they are by flirting with you. At first it's intoxicating to receive this kind of attention, making it hard to stop the behavior that's causing it.

It's a dead end road, though, so force yourself to stop after 5-10 minutes.

Persistence

It was the 2005 Pickup Artist Summit. I had organized it and it was to be the first time that all of the top pickup artists in the world gathered in one place to share their ideas and methods.

Because of different feuds, it was the last event of its kind.

My star was on the rise. I'd gone from being a nobody to being the student of the masters. I had a lot to prove.

Of course, there were also one hundred spectators who had come along. Every club we went to was lined with aspiring pickup artists who wanted to see what we could do.

We stood on the patio of the Saddle Ranch in Hollywood. Three girls were standing near the railing with three of my pickup friends talking to them.

Almost.

One of them rudely had her back turned to my friend, who just couldn't crack her. He laughed and came up to me.

"Try that one. I can't get a word out of her."

I glanced around at the spectators watching and started heading towards the girl. This would be impressive if I could pull it off.

I addressed her, but she wouldn't turn around. I told her a quick story and received no response.

I'd never met a girl this cold before, but I couldn't fail in front of all these people. I told her another story. And then another and another. Nothing. No response.

Finally I told her a funny story, and around the corner of her face I saw her crack a smile. She still hadn't looked at me once, but I could tell I was getting to her.

"Ok, that's it," I said, "here I am entertaining you and being a good guy and you're ignoring me? I see you laughing. I caught you. I'm out of here."

I turned around, knowing exactly what would happen. I felt a hand on my shoulder.

"No, wait!"

She was smiling. From then on she was very friendly and warm. After the club went to dinner with our friends and then she came back up to our house with me.

The reason she was so cold at first was because a creepy ex boyfriend was calling her every three minutes trying to find out where she was. She was in a bad mood and had no desire to talk to guys.

However, I was able to show that I was different than that guy and she loved me for it.

My point is this - it's not over until it's over. Unless she specifically tells you to leave her alone, don't leave. And if she says it too early, wait for her to say it again.

If you follow my advice to become the kind of guy that girls want in their lives, you'll have to push through that initial wall sometimes.

And this doesn't just go for the initial opener, either. If she doesn't kiss you one day, try again the next time you see her. If she's willingly keeping you company, you're still in the game.

I feel like this is a good point to give this obligatory warning: this does not in any way mean to force yourself on a girl. If you try to kiss a girl and she says no, then back off. If she says to leave, then leave. Don't insult her, just walk away and tell her it was nice to meet her.

Delivering

Now that you've convinced her that you're a worthwhile guy to know, it's time to prove it. As long as you still know the girl, you're still in the delivering phase.

All it requires is being the most amazing guy she's ever met.

Keeping it up is easy, because the idea is to actually BE the most amazing guy, not just act like him by reciting lines that you've memorized. This is why a lot of people become pickup artists, only to find frustration in the fact that they can't actually keep a girl.

On the other hand, I'm excellent at keeping girls because I have designed my life to be as interesting and exciting as possible (for me as well as girls who come into it), while eliminating anything I do that could be construed as jealous, needy, insecure, or creepy.

This may seem like a considerable amount of effort just to meet girls, but you'll surely find that it pays off in many other ways.

When I began focusing on the principles I'm about to teach you, I found that not only did my success with women increase dramatically, but so did my relationships with my friends and family, my business improved noticeably, and I became a happier person.

In this stage, I use almost no lines or canned routines. The idea is to get her to know who you really are. One exception is my version of the 100% Perfect Girl routine, which I adapted from Style's version. I like this because it's simply telling her a story I heard (often I've already explained that I'm a pickup artist, and use this as an example of a routine).

No matter the context, it's always effective to set the tone for the relationship and for her to realize that she has one chance to "win" you.

Another routine I particularly like is The Cube. It's based on a psychology study, and was adapted for pickup a long time ago. I tend to tell them that it's a pickup routine like the 100% Perfect Girl story and they like it because it demonstrates that I'm getting to know them as well.

Girls love hearing about themselves, and showing that you understand them is very attractive. Both of these routines are available at the end of the book.

Other than those routines, your conversations should be like conversations that you have with your friends, peppered with occasional flirting and stories about your life. If you're reading this book, your life is probably at least 18 years long. Hopefully in those tens of thousands of hours of life, you've had enough interesting experiences to share.

Don't be afraid to talk about her as well. It's important for her to share her stories with you. Ask her about what she wants out of life, and about her future. If you disagree with her opinion, let her know! I've had several girls tell me that they like how I never back down from arguments just to appease them.

If the argument is going nowhere, don't let it drag out too long. Show her that proving her wrong isn't that important to you, and say "well… maybe we'll never know for sure" and change the subject.

There are a few traits that all girls find inherently attractive, so you may as well embody all of them.

Confidence

Think of ten people you admire. How many of them are confident? My guess would be all of them. Confidence is probably the sexiest quality a man can have, and is surprisingly easy to cultivate and express. One of the easiest ways to become confident is to act as though you're confident.

When you see that people accept your confidence, and that it improves your performance in all areas of life, you will naturally become confident. This is one area that it's ok to fake because you're genuinely working towards it.

Don't think you have anything to be confident about? You're wrong.

You're here, and you're alive. You made it. Sure there are some things wrong with your life, but that could be said about almost anyone. If you're reading this book (and I assume you are), then you've already shown that you're confident. It takes a lot of self assuredness to admit that you need help with women and to actually take action on it.

When I taught workshops with Mystery I was constantly humbled by the men who would admit that there was something wrong in their life and take drastic steps like signing up to learn from us to fix it.

If you share that you're learning about this with women, they will perceive it as you being confident as long as you say it confidently!

Think about things that have gone well in your life. They went well because YOU made them go well. Even things that seem lucky—you allowed them to happen and probably took some action to spawn them.

Be proud of who you are and of the decisions you've made.

Never apologize for yourself, unless you do something that you know was wrong (for example, if you elbow a girl in the face by accident, please apologize).

Bad forms of apologizing can take the form of "Hey, SORRY to bother you, but can you help settle a bet," where you're directly saying that you're sorry.

It can also be revealed by indirectly expressing that you're sorry. When I tell girls about pickup, I tell them matter of factly that I used to be bad with women, I learned, and now I'm good. I don't make excuses for being bad—I just say that's how it was.

If you say, "Yeah, I'm learning this pickup stuff. I don't know if it really works or whatever, but my friend told me about it so I'm just reading it for fun," you are telling her subconsciously that you're ashamed of what you're doing.

No one wants to be around someone who is ashamed of their actions, as this is the direct opposite of being confident. Become hyper aware of what everything you say says about you, because everything you say DOES say something about you. It doesn't all have to be good, but 95% of it should be, and that last 5% are still mistakes.

How about asking for a date?

"If you're free sometime, maybe we could go on a date?"

That statement is so full of uncertainty that it's sickening. Girls don't want to hear that. Sometimes I'll call girls and just tell them what we're doing.

"Hey, be ready in an hour. I'm picking you up and we're doing something really fun."

Some people are embarrassed because they have crappy cars, and they make excuses for them.

"I'm sorry the car's a mess. I'm actually going to get a new one soon…"

She doesn't care what kind of car you have, so any justification you're doling out is clearly only coming from your own insecurity.

I can't tell you how many pickup artists I know who drive old crappy cars that are broken. It never slows them down.

Some even consider it a badge of pride, as they are too smart to spend money trying to impress girls with a brand new car.

These sorts of things work for you doubly well because she's used to guys being embarrassed about having a bad car, and she's also used to rich losers trying to impress her with their cars. When you roll around in a 91 Ford Taurus and don't even mention it, she'll wonder where your confidence comes from.

Confidence also takes the form of strong opinions. The subject or opinion isn't nearly as important as the conviction. I have tons of these:

- Eating sugar will kill you, so I don't eat any of it.
- Dropping out of school is a great idea.
- I want to have a billion dollars and a submarine.
- I'm going to climb Mount Everest.
- Drinking from plastic cups is gross.
- Tap water is better than bottled water.
- I'm not paying for dates.

She may share all of these thoughts or none of them. What's relevant is that I am a staunch believer in each one, and I will never back down. Don't be the guy in this conversation:

He says, "I hate scary movies."

"Really? I love them."

"Oh. I like some of them. Which ones do you like?"

"28 Days Later and The Grudge were good."

"Yeah, I like those ones too."

See how he's totally flipped on his convictions just to gain her favor? She sees right through it and he has achieved the opposite of his goal. She now knows that he's not confident and is pandering to her tastes.

You don't need to start an argument either. People who argue a lot are generally not very confident. Here's a better way to handle the situation:

"I hate scary movies."

"Really? I love them."

"Oh, I can't stand them. They're never as scary as I expect, but I get all freaked out anticipating the scary parts, so I never actually enjoy the movie."

"Ooh… I love that feeling."

"Well, hopefully we have some movie tastes in common, or we'll never get along. Do you like 70s midget porn?"

Here I've shown that I'm willing to back up my opinion, but that I'm not insecure enough about it to try to convince her that there's something wrong with her opinion. By admitting that I get scared, I show a bit of vulnerability without being embarrassed about it. Since it's no fun to talk about how we don't have this in common, I end the conversation with a joke.

Being confident, bordering on cocky is a good thing. However, it should always be used to raise you up, not to put others down. Most cocky guys that women encounter are constantly putting other guys down. This is tiresome and makes her wonder if the confidence is genuine or not.

I am extremely confident and cocky, and girls know it. In fact, I'm quick to tell them that I am very self centered and cocky.

Several girls have told me that they can't figure out why they like it when I'm cocky but hate when other guys are. I know why—it's because I build up myself, as well as other people, and I never put people down. I like to talk about how great my friends are, or how wonderful my family is.

I say that I'm great, but it's because my mother did such a good job raising me, and that I was fortunate to have such great friends.

I might speak poorly of segments of the population ("I just don't understand how people eat junk food all day. It's so dumb"), but I'll never say something like, "Tom's such an idiot. He eats all that junk food all day, but I'm smart enough to eat healthy."

If you actively try to become and act more confident, you will soon become more confident than you could ever imagine being. Also, you'll be so tuned into confidence that you'll detect when girls aren't very confident. When you notice this, it makes you feel a lot more at ease talking to them, and makes it fun to try to make them feel comfortable enough with you to get their confidence back.

Humor

Having a sense of humor is important. You don't need to crack jokes constantly, but you need to be able to make her laugh from time to time.

First, NEVER make self deprecating jokes. Admitting faults is fine, but making jokes about them will make her wonder if you're actually confident or not. These jokes are usually made due to insecurity.

If it's a fault she's known about for a while, it's ok to talk about it in a way that clearly demonstrates that you are not embarassed or insecure.

For example, I have an awful sense of direction. I've tried to improve it, but progress has been thin. I don't really care, since I have a GPS, and girls know that I'm not concerned about it.

Once in a while I can make a joke like, "You'd better drive. If I navigate we'll end up in Russia" without making her wonder if I'm self conscious.

Don't try to imitate other people's sense of humor too much. Focus on things that you think are funny, and try to articulate what makes them funny to you.

The key is to be authentic in all areas of attracting girls. If you try to imitate someone else's sense of humor, it will be obvious to the girl. It's far better to take the time to cultivate your own sense of humor.

Written jokes aren't very funny. Don't repeat comedians' jokes. This always comes off fake, as if you're putting on an act.

You don't have to be funny often. It's better to be reserved and say something funny once a week than to say mildly funny things several times a day.

I had a friend in college who was usually rather stoic, but would occasionally say something funny. The contrast against his normal serious demeanor helped make the jokes seem even funnier.

Practice being funny around your friends and family. See what they respond to. You'll probably find that most of humor is in the timing, which is something easier learned through practice than explanation.

Whatever you do, NEVER laugh at your own jokes until everyone else is laughing. Even then, a polite chuckle is all it takes. The ONLY reason people laugh at their own jokes is to try to induce others to laugh, whether consciously or unconsciously.

Sometimes something will be so incredibly funny that you'll have to laugh. As long as you're making a sincere effort not to, don't worry about it too much.

If people don't laugh at your jokes, the jokes aren't that funny.

Don't take it personally, it just means that you need more practice being funny. Don't worry – they heard your joke, and they understood it. There's no need for clarification.

Don't be one of those people who follows up with, "What? I thought it was funny."

Even hilarious people like me make bad jokes once in a while. Just move on and don't react to the silence.

When you comment on people not laughing, it creates the most awkward of all moments. She didn't find it funny, but can't say that, so she has to force a laugh or assure you that it is funny. Meanwhile, she's just thinking about how insecure you seem.

Laugh at her jokes.

If they're not that funny, then make a decision. Either you're not interested in her, or you're going to put up with bad jokes and laugh. Your job is to make her feel comfortable around you, and that includes laughing at her stupid jokes. It seems like a double standard, and it is – but deal with it.

Another nuance: never tell her that you're "just kidding". She knows when you're just kidding, because she's not a total idiot.

When people say things like, "Yeah, he wishes he could shoot a crossbow like me. Haha... Just kidding" it once again displays insecurity.

If you aren't very funny by nature, then don't try to be a clown. It's better to not make jokes than to make bad jokes, so practice with your friends until you know that your jokes will hit.

The one difference in humor delivery with girls, is that they respond to their emotions, rather than logic. Guys tend to prefer logical deadpan jokes, while girls like jokes that are expressed with a lot of emotion and will make them giggle.

To achieve this effect, make sure that you vary the tone of your voice as well as the look on your face. If a person in your funny story was surprised, make a surprised face as you talk about him.

Individuality

Every guy is the same to girls.

You wear blue jeans, a white and blue button down shirt, and trendy sneakers. You like football, beer, and cars. You're going to talk to her about her job, your job, parties you've been to, and possibly what you're doing on spring break.

This is what she believes, and she's waiting for you to confirm her suspicions.

Our culture leads us to believe that to be attractive we need to fit in and emulate others, but this couldn't be farther from the truth. The more different you are (without being scary), the more attractive you are.

Note that being different by conforming to an alternative stereotype doesn't count as being different (I'm talking about hippies, Goths, and emo kids here).

Her prince charming isn't a cookie cutter man of any type – he is an individual who has his own opinions and hobbies.

Rarity is always prized. If she feels like you're just one guy who is mostly the same as everyone else, she will always be looking to replace you. It will be easy for her to do so.

However, if you are one in a million and she's never met ANYONE like you before, she will cling to you for dear life. This is true even if the things that make you unique aren't necessarily exactly what she's looking for.

Rolex makes some of the best watches and most expensive watchs in the world. One particular model they make is called the "Daytona".

A limited run of these watches was created with minor differences, the most significant being slightly different hour markers that are thick rectangles instead of thin lines.

It's called the "Paul Newman Daytona".

This watch sells for many times more than an indentical rolex with the normal markers.

Why? Is it because watch collectors love rectangular markers? No, it's because it's rare.

When a girl has a rare date or boyfriend, she has to seriously consider losing him. She makes the decision knowing full well that she will never meet another guy like you again.

That's hard to walk away from.

Hobbies

Girls are attracted to men with unusual hobbies. This is primarily because it's an example of individuality, and it gives her something to learn about, and a way to get into "your world".

Chances are that you already have some different hobbies. It really doesn't matter what they are, as long as they aren't mainstream.

Some prime examples of good hobbies would be flying helicopters, painting oil paintings, singing opera, or mountain climbing. These are different and fascinating to most people.

However, even more mundane hobbies will do. For example, I learned how to solve the Rubik's cube. It sounds extremely nerdy (and it is, really), but girls never fail to be impressed when they see me solve it.

I like to do crazy daredevil things. I once built a swing that could swing over my 13th story balcony. At the same time, my neighbor was having an amazing party filled with the hottest women in Austin. To give you an idea of the caliber of this party, Mel Gibson was one of the guests.

I went over, started talking about my swing, and next thing I knew, every one of the hot girls was on my balcony wanting to try the swing. I took the spotlight from Mel Gibson, and even he followed everyone over.

No girl says that she dreams of a man who builds swings off his balcony, but the contrast between my interests and the boring guys at the party (incidentally, Mel was an amazing storyteller) was so overwhelming that they couldn't help but be drawn into my world.

Even taking mundane hobbies and becoming a real expert in them is attractive.

Most guys like beer. My friend AceOfHearts is a beer aficionado who literally takes out a piece of paper and reviews every beer he drinks.

That sort of bizarre behavior triggers curiosity in everyone, beautiful women included.

You probably already have interesting hobbies. Think about the things you like to do, and evaluate which ones girls don't know a lot about or don't hear a lot about.

If you don't have interesting hobbies, pick some up! I don't think that you should do many things for the sole purpose of attracting women, but getting new hobbies can be rewarding in a lot of ways.

Remember that girls love to tell their friends about the guys they're dating. If you have a unique hobby that she can talk about, it makes "her guy" more appealing than her friends' boyfriends. This is a powerful social bargaining chip for her.

"Oh, the guy I'm seeing now is really cool. He runs marathons."

This is very different from:

"Oh, the guy I'm seeing now is really cool."

Dress

Your clothes are telling a story about you to everyone who sees you. What are they saying?

If you're like most guys, they're saying "I'm a boring idiot who's afraid to express himself." If you're a bit trendier they might be saying "My look is important to me, so I look at what other people are wearing and copy them."

If neither of those stories is what you want people thinking of you, then it's time to change. Mystery first came up with this idea and calls it "peacocking."

To be honest, I had limited faith in it like most people who first hear the concept. Then I went to Hollywood and saw Mystery wear the most absurd outfits.

He wore platform boots, huge hats, strange plastic backpacks, goggles, and even a men's dress. The reaction was amazing – girls treated him like a rock star.

Experiment with different styles of dress, and even wear some items that are meant for costumes. Maybe you feel comfortable in pajamas like Hugh Hefner. Why not wear those all the time?

I like to have a signature item that people will identify with me. I used to wear a feather boa when I lived in Hollywood. I wore this boa so much that on any given day you could walk down Sunset Boulevard and see feathers that had dropped from nights before. Now I wear a sequined hat every single day.

Not only does it stand out and induce women to come up to me to start a conversation, it makes me much more memorable. All of the bouncers remember me and let me in, but forget my more plainly dressed friends. If girls see me out twice, they often come up to me the second time and tell me that they saw me wearing my hat before.

I'm personally very bad at remembering people, but they always remember me because of my hat.

You wouldn't believe the mileage I've gotten out of this $20 hat. Don't be afraid of items that may lead people to believe you're gay. Girls always know somehow that I'm straight, and they assume that I'm brave to wear such an outlandish item.

Regardless of what you wear, it's important that it fits well. Ill fitting clothes look awkward and sloppy.

Get a girl to help you pick out clothes (seriously, what girl doesn't want to go shopping?) or even ask people who work at the store. Most guys wear clothes that are too large or baggy, so err on the side of too tight if necessary.

Go for a look that is coherent and fits your personality. If you're a reserved businessman, don't spike your hair into a mohawk and wear torn jeans.

Try a well cut suit with a flourescent yellow tie. You always want to be edgy, but you want it to describe your personality.

Have your whole wardrobe go together, like courses in a meal. You don't want to have some cool trendy clothes, and then have the rest of your shirts be free T-shirts you got at a trade show.

If you can't afford to buy a whole new wardrobe, however, just focus on the basics. Get a good pair of jeans that fit you well, a decent pair of shoes, and a few shirts that fit well.

And of course, get that one signature item that you always wear. As I write this for the revised edition of Make Her Chase You, I'm on a trip around the world with only a tiny backpack full of the essentials. My hat made the cut.

You will undoubtedly face criticism from some of your friends or family at your new look. Ignore them. They don't know what's attractive and what isn't, and probably aren't attracting ANYONE with their clothes.

An interesting option for pants is to get a pair of women's jeans if you're skinny. This is a much more common practice than you'd imagine. Girls' clothes tend to be less bland than clothes for men, so for $20 you can get an interesting pair of jeans with a good cut. The one caveat? Watch out for tiny useless pockets.

Eccentricities

I wouldn't advise that you go out and make a concerted effort to affect new mannerisms, but realize that differences between you and the norm are by definition the things that make you you, so they should be celebrated.

Never be embarrassed about anything you do differently, as it will reek of insecurity.

If you are ashamed of your unique characteristics, then you are embarrassed about who you are as a person. Girls can read this from a mile away.

A good example is drinking. I've never had a drink, and never plan to. I personally believe that it's a rather stupid thing to do.

When I tell some people, they insist that they'd feel awkward without a drink in their hand, or they come up with ways to avoid letting girls know they don't drink.

I don't make a moral lecture out of it, but I'm more than happy to tell girls that I don't drink, and why.

I also don't really swear. I don't think that there's anything particularly wrong with profanity, just that it's classier not to use it. Rather than try to fit in by sounding like everyone else, I use my own vocabulary and thus set myself apart from the common man that girls are so sick of.

Tyler is a redhead, and naturally very pale white. When girls would bring up how pasty he was, he never got defensive about it.

Instead he would go on the offensive telling girls that tanning causes skin cancer and that he's an aristocrat. Aristocrats are pale, he says, because they stay inside rather than work on the field.

It's such a hilarious answer that girls couldn't help but be intrigued—and maybe feel a bit self conscious about their tans.

One of my recent girlfriends cited two different events as the time that I won her over:

The first was when she was hanging out with me and I lectured her for 10 minutes about the importance of getting cryogenically frozen after death. It was so random and I seemed so into it that she was charmed.

The next was when I decided that I absolutely had to see the movie Road Trip with her.

We couldn't find it, so she wanted to settle on another movie. Instead I drove to Wal-Mart, got a motorized old person cart, put her on my lap, and drove around looking for the movie.

Acting like this is interesting. It awakens a part of her brain that hasn't been spoken to in years. It invites curiousity and makes her wonder what's coming next.

Don't be afraid to exaggerate your mannerisms to become more memorable. If a girl sees that I occasionally eat fruit, it seems normal. If I am always carrying an orange around she wonders why I do that and it becomes part of my character.

If Popeye occasionally ate spinach, no one would notice, but since he does it all the time, we associate it with him and he becomes more memorable.

Drive

Let's say that two planes are leaving one afternoon. One is leaving from Omaha, Nebraska and is headed for Costa Rica. The other one is leaving from Los Angeles and is heading for Seattle, Washington. You have a ticket on each plane, and can choose to be magically transported to the airport in LA or in Nebraska. Which do you choose?

Stupid question, right? The location of the terminal is totally irrelevant. The plane going to Costa Rica is a better choice because Costa Rica is probably a lot more fun than Seattle.

Girls feel the same way.

They don't really care where you are now; they just care where you're going and how motivated you are to get there.

Everyone has driving passions in their lives. I want to be a billionaire, buy my own island, and go to space. What's interesting is that having drive to get my goals is a more potent attractor than what my goals actually are.

In other words, a guy who is working towards getting an island is often times more exciting than one who already has an island and is tired of it.

I've seen many girls get bored of their boyfriends who make six figures a year and are content to keep earning that much and watch TV all day. It's not exciting.

You should talk openly about your goals with passion and motivation. Tell her about things that you know she won't care about, like your aspirations to be a chess champion. Chess isn't interesting to most girls, but your quest to become a champion will interest her.

If you don't have goals, get some! They don't have to be about making money or getting rich. They should be about whatever you're interested in.

For a while I lived in a penthouse in downtown Austin. It was one of the top ten condos in the whole city.

One day I decided that I was sick of having so much stuff. I wanted to live simply with as few posessions and responsibilities as possible.

I sold everything I owned, including the condo and my car.

I then bought a very small RV and parked it on the side of the road near my favorite restaraunt. Not even in a trailer park—just on the side of the road. I lived there for nine months.

Was it a problem to bring girls back to the tiny RV? Not at all—they were intrigued by my drive to be totally portable and live a simple life, so they loved the RV.

Take stock of her goals. Most people have goals in their lives, and if you can relate to her goals and help motivate her, she'll love you for it.

I remember a girl in Hollywood who waited tables at my favorite club. I asked her what she wanted to do when she grew up, and she told me she wanted to be a cartoonist. I immediately launched into a speech about how she had to follow her dreams and just do it.

I'm not sure that she ever did, but I know she enjoyed the fantasy of it that I created and the faith I had in her.

Excitement and Optimism

Being excited about your goals isn't enough. You should be excited about lots of things.

The world that we live in is a truly astounding place. Whether you believe a man in the sky made it or that it evolved over an eternity, the result is something incredible.

Unlike all the other species on Earth, we not only have the ability to think and move our thumbs, but we also have computers, cars, airplanes, whole grain bread, and a bunch of other amazing things.

No matter what your situation is, you are incredibly fortunate to be alive.

When I think about this, I get excited.

Most people in this country, and possibly the world, are bored. They do the same routine every day, and they see the same things. They meet new people occasionally and bore each other with lame conversation.

Long gone is the childlike wonder for the world that causes little kids smile all the time.

When you meet a new girl, realize that these are the people that she deals with every day. She is dying to meet someone different who's excited about his life. When you're excited it's contagious, and girls can't help but share your excitement.

This may be the most important piece of advice I've given you so far. If you can control the excitement level of the conversation, you will get the girl every time.

I've had so many girls tell me that when they're with me they feel happy, that they can do anything, and that they're never bored, but they don't know why.

I know why.

It's because I'm an excited person, and I like to share that enthusiasm for life with other people.

Movies tell us that cool people are stoic rocks of emotion who walk around with poker faces. This simply isn't true. All of the coolest people I know are extremely excited about life, their projects, and seeing other people succeed.

Cool people only act "cool" in emergency situations, and you should too. If you're trapped in someone's volcano lair... that's the time to transcend your emotions and be cool. When you're meeting women, it's time to be fun and exciting.

When I moved to Hollywood I was shocked at how excited each of the pickup artists was. Each one was excited about our new house in Hollywood, excited about his projects, and generally excited about life.

None of those people, the most seductive people in the world, were quiet and reserved. That's just not how it works in the real world.

I used to eat all of my meals at the vegan restaurant across from my RV. It's the exact kind of food I like to eat, and I can eat as much as I want for a good price. The menu changed every day, all the employees knew me, and my friends frequently joined me to eat there.

Even though most girls I meet aren't vegan or even healthy eaters, they can't help but enjoy my enthusiasm for the restaurant. They join me eating there and get into it as well.

It's vital to be both excited about life, but also be optimistic about the future. Since there's no cost to doing so, and there could be some benefit, why not assume everything is going to work perfectly?

I attribute a lot of my success in many areas of my life to my undying optimism. It's surprisingly easy to become an optimistic person, and it's one of the main traits that determines whether or not someone is considered to be charismatic.

Many years ago, I wasn't always happy and optimistic. I had my share of negative thoughts and worries. Then one day, for no real good reason, I decided that any time I had a negative thought, I would immediately try to find something uplifting about it.

The good thought didn't have to outweigh the bad – it just had to be there. I resolved to try this for one month.

For the first month it was a cumbersome process, but I stuck with it. If I got a flat tire, I would think about how at least I got to get some fresh air while I changed it. If I lost money (I used to be a professional gambler), I would think about how lucky I was to be able to lose money and still be ok. If I lost a bet to a friend, I'd be glad that he felt good about winning.

After a month I decided that I liked this process, so I tried it for another month.

When the third month rolled around, I realized that I had forgotten all about my happy experiment. For a second I was disappointed, but then I realized that I was still doing it – it had just become automatic.

Since then it's been easy to maintain. I don't even think about it anymore, and I find myself only having positive thoughts. Since the day I started I have been an incredibly happy person and I can't think of a single bad thing that's happened to me since.

It's not much of a stretch to realize that girls notice that I'm always happy and positive, and want to be around me because of it.

If she gets bad news, or is in a bad mood, use this as an opportunity to cheer her up, not an opportunity to complain with her. Let her vent if that's what she needs to do, respond appropriately ("I'm sorry to hear that..."), and then change the subject. "Hey, that really sucks. So how was your day besides totally wrecking your car?"

Saying something like that is usually funny enough that she'll take the bait and get in a better mood.

Try the 30 day happiness challenge for yourself. All you have to do is notice when you get upset, and think of ONE positive aspect about the thing that's making you upset.

How Good do you Have to Be?

I spent over a year without being single. I had a long term relationship with one girl, started seeing another girl (which, of course I was open about with her), stopped seeing her, and then kept seeing the new girl.

During that year, other than hosting Tazeroke (an event I invented where people sing karaoke and I taze them with an 800,000 volt stun baton if they're bad), I didn't go to a club once.

My game was rusty. Really rusty.

A friend of mine was opening a club in Austin, so I had to go out and check it out. In my tiny RV closet I had two shirts that were appropriate for an upscale club. I put one on and headed out.

It was opening night and the club was packed. There was a mob of people outside trying to get in. Inside were the most beautiful girls in all of Austin and a lot of the coolest guys as well.

I stood around chatting with my friends when I saw two girls about to walk by us. One was a tall blond with curly hair and the other was a short Asian girl.

"Hey guys, give me a boost. I need to climb up there and show those cage dancers how to be sexy."

They laugh and I start telling them my stories. It's going well, but not great. I don't have that punch that you develop by going out regularly.

They're not leaving, but I can tell they're not totally thrilled either. I decide to break out a new idea I had come up with—talk about something inappropriate within the first few minutes to really catch their attention.

"You know, you guys better watch out. I'm a feminist and I believe in equal rights, including the right to be slapped. Keep being sassy and you could be getting a close up of this guy."

I waved my hand in the air.

"You would never slap me!" said the blonde.

"Oh yeah I would. I've slapped many girls."

"He's lying," said the Asian girl.

"I'm not lying. In fact, I had this friend who kept doing something annoying. I told her that if she did it one more time, I'd slap her."

"Did she do it?"

"Yep."

"Did you slap her?"

"Well, I gave her one more warning. I said 'look, I'm giving you this warning because you're my friend, but I will really slap you if you do it again.' She sized me up and did it one more time. Then I slapped her."

"Oh my god. What did she do?"

"She took it."

"I would be so pissed at you if you slapped me," said the blonde.

I switched to a serious voice and looked her in the eye with a small smile.

"No. You'd love it."

After that they were there to stay. I introduced them to my friends and told them some more stories. I noticed that my stories weren't getting the big reactions I was used to. I was out of practice, but it was still fun.

"Oh my god! Do you paint your nails!?"

I paint them silver usually, and that night was no exception.

"Wow! They're really good. Who does them for you?"

"I do. I dated a girl whose mom owned a salon and she taught me how."

I then launched into an explanation of how to properly paint your nails. I explained it in excruciating detail, which made them laugh because most guys don't know these things.

"But... I like manicures too. I've always wanted to go to Cuba Libre on Tuesdays. They have manicurists at the bar, so you can go out and get a manicure."

"Wow, that sounds so cool!"

"Yeah, you and I will go next week and get our nails done."

"Ok."

This is an important point here. I've playfully suggested us meeting up. Because I say it playfully she cannot possibly refuse, even if she doesn't want to go. If she does it will seem very rude and not fun.

It's not a firm commitment by any measure, but it's a step in the right direction.

I immediately changed the topic so that she would wonder if I was serious and not think that I was overly interested in going out with her.

After about an hour, my voice was totally shot. I decided to go sit on a couch with some of my friends. I quickly excused myself and sat and drank water for an hour.

The club was an amazing sight. They had hired live drummers to run around drumming to the music, so I zoned out, enjoyed the music and watched people dance.

Finally at two a.m. the club was beginning to wind down. I thought about getting the blonde's number, but I honestly didn't think I'd done well enough. I'm used to delivering really high level game, and I could identify a lot of mistakes I'd made over the night.

I was too eager to tell some stories. I didn't change the subject enough. I didn't touch her enough or talk about anything sexual.

She walked by where I was sitting, apparently looking for her coat.

I knew better than that. She was hoping I'd ask for her number.

"Hey, it was really good talking to you. I had to come sit over here because my voice is wrecked. I haven't been out in a long time."

"I know... my voice is shot too... Hey... are we going to get our nails done?"

Bingo.

"Yeah, I can't go this week, but let's do it next week."

I hand her my phone and she puts in her number.

The next week I call her while I'm wandering around campus looking for my RV. I was filming a promo for a small TV appearance as a dating coach and in my haste to get to the station, I'd totally forgotten where I'd parked.

I chatted for a few minutes and then told her I'd call her on Thursday when they did the manicures at the club.

That Thursday we got our nails done. One of the nail technicians (yeah, that's what they call themselves) asked if we were a couple.

Before I could make a funny comment she answered quickly, "Oh no, nothing like that. Just friends."

Normally I would ignore this completely because a girl's actions mean a lot more than her words. But I was already not happy with my performance the other day so I wasn't expecting much.

Don't get me wrong—I was still doing most things right, I just wasn't on fire like I prefer to be.

"Hey, my friends and I are going to go eat miracle berries. Want to come?"

Miracle berries are these weird African berries I'd heard about on the internet. When you eat one it coats your tongue with a protein that blocks all sour flavors for twenty minutes. You can eat lemons and limes and they taste like candy.

She was intrigued so she came along. The miracle berries were amazing, and I knew that if nothing else, this would be the most interesting "date" she'd ever been on.

She drove me back to my RV where she had picked me up, and I got out. I should have gone for the kiss or invited her in, but I hesitated and it was too late.

Two days later she called me and told me that she was at Magnolia Cafe, a 24 hour diner, with some friends, and asked if I wanted to go. I needed a break from work so I headed over.

When I got there I saw that she was with a guy and a girl. Perfect. A guy to eclipse and a girl to win over.

It didn't take long. A few stories in and the guy had stopped trying to tell stories because his couldn't compare. I could tell that the girl really wanted for me to hook up with the blonde girl.

"We're lesbians. She's GREAT in bed, you know," she said jokingly and winked at me.

When that happened I knew that the blonde had told her that she was interested in me.

After we finished eating, I offered to give them rides back to their cars since they took cabs from the club. Once I dropped off the friends I was going to tell the blonde to come back to the RV.

My plot was foiled, however, when I found out that the two girls had driven together.

I went back to the RV alone. I was pretty happy with my performance that night... the one time at the club and the one night with her getting manicures had warmed me up quite a bit.

I got under the covers and began to drift off when I heard my phone ring.

"Hello?"

"Hey. Can I come over?"

"Sure."

Sometimes it's easy to get caught up in pickup and believe that you have to be a master pickup artist who performs perfectly every time. That's not true.

In this situation I did a lot of things right, but I did a lot of things wrong as well. The simple fact is that you just have to be better than every other guy.

Fortunately for you they're doing almost everything wrong, so that isn't all that difficult on a task. Don't be afraid of making a few mistakes—focus on doing the best you can at all times, and that should be enough.

You could actually ignore about half the stuff in this book and still become very good with women. The reason I try to cover every last aspect is to give you more opportunites to do things right.

Do Looks Matter?

Only to us.

As you're quite aware, looks are the most important factor to us menfolk. There's a reason that most pornography used by men is visual, either pictures or video.

Most of us require a great personality in our female companions as well, but without her looks we don't care too much about her personality. Don't beat yourself up about it, that's just how things are.

Women are different, though. If they watch porn, they do it out of amusement rather than excitement.

When they fantasize, they close their eyes and use their imaginations. They consume romance novels by the truckload rather than the *Playboy* magazines we "read".

The fundamental sexual difference between women and men is that men are turned on visually while women are turned on through language and emotion. It's hard for us to grasp this since we can't really relate, so deep down inside most of us think that our looks matter.

Women hardly care what we look like.

They do care about how well groomed we are and how we dress, because they read into these things as indicators of our personality. They're usually right, which is why it's important to be well groomed and to dress in a way that reflects your personality.

There are good looking men, bad looking men, and average looking men. Ninety percent of men are average looking, which is good enough. Five percent are so good looking that women consider them rare and will be especially attracted to them, and five percent are bad enough looking that they will start off at a disadvantage (this is hardly insurmountable—I've seen some extremely ugly guys become successful).

The one significant advantage that good looking guys have over us average looking guys is that they think looks are important, and know that they are good looking. This typically breeds a very confident attitude which is extremely sexy to women.

This confidence attracts women, which they chalk up to their natural good looks, and thus the myth is perpetuated.

One very strange phenomenon that I and others have noticed is that when girls are attracted to you because of your game, they will think that you are physically attractive.

Before getting into the game I received few if any compliments on my looks, which I expect. I'm certainly not in the bottom five percent, but as you've probably noticed from my picture, I'm about average looking at best (incidentally, guys have a hard time judging how attractive each other are because 90% of us fit in that middle category).

Once I got into the game, I started getting compliments like they were going out of fashion. Girls would tell me how hot I was. When they were to guess what my job was, many would guess model or actor!

Grooming

Grooming is very important to women, so let's get up on it.

The gravest issue we face is hair maintenance. Unlike (most) women, pores all over our bodies are hair sprouting factories which occasionally need to be put into check.

Eyebrows

Pluck your eyebrows. It makes your face appear cleaner and "opens up your eyes". I have no idea what that means exactly, but Katya was a makeup artist and she always said that.

The most important part is between your brows. Get some tweezers and individually pluck hairs by grasping the hair as close to the skin as possible and pulling. If a girl or a professional does it, they will also pull extra hairs around the brow to slightly shape it. This looks great but hurts a lot, unlike between the eyebrows.

Armpits

I'll bet you didn't know that you had to bring blades anywhere near this area. You do. Trimming is a minimum, but you may want to consider shaving. Every girl I've ever asked has preferred shaved armpits.

If it sounds a bit too feminine for you, consider this: bodybuilders shave their armpits, and they're pretty manly. That's how Mystery convinced me that it was a good idea.

Chest and Back

Chest and back hair are ok left alone if you'd like to remain only moderately high maintenance. Trimming chest hair is easy and looks good.

I have no back hair, but I believe that waxing is probably the only option there. Most women don't have problems with chest and back hair, so feel free to leave them alone.

Skin

The quality of your skin can make a difference as well. As a disclaimer, I used to have moderate acne and it never interfered with my game. There was also a pickup artist friend of mine who had bad acne and did just fine.

The main reason I'm including this is because it's an insecurity many people have and I happen to know the best ways to deal with it.

The absolute best way to deal with acne is through your diet. When I stopped eating sugar, white flour, and all animal products, my skin cleared up completely with no additional work necessary.

It was amazing, and is only one of many reasons that I'd passionately reccomend that you go vegan (read my personal blog at *www.betterthanyourboyfriend.com* for more information).

If you won't go vegan, the next best option is benzoyl peroxide.

The highest quality product at the cheapest price (go figure!) lives at *www.acne.org* along with some great information on clearing your acne. It didn't work 100% for me, but I noticed a drastic improvement within a few weeks of using it.

I know we're now encroaching on the realm of *Queer Eye for the Straight Guy* here, but I've also found that using a facial moisturizer makes a noticable difference.

Apply it every day after you shave (or if you don't shave everyday, right after you dry your face after your shower), and you'll notice that your skin is smoother, softer, and seems to glow a bit.

I frequently forget to do this, but if you're dedicated to good skin, it's probably worth a try.

One last skin tip, while I'm at it. My ex girlfriend had some of the best skin I'd even encountered during my time here on earth. Her trick was to cover her face in Vaseline before going to sleep. In fact, during the winter she would wear gloves with vaseline in them and socks with vaseline in them to bed.

This seems extremely strange to me, but I can't argue with the results. She had great skin.

The Chase

One of the most important things you'll find in pickup is that you must encourage the woman to chase you. Hence the name of this book.

Too often men try to play the role of romantic pursuer, only to get resented and left for a man that she can chase after. This is unattractive behavior and is sure to turn any woman off.

My female friends frequently laugh with me about guys who go overboard trying to pursue them. On the other hand, when one of them can't get the guy, she can't stop telling me how amazing he is.

The obvious solution is to act like she's chasing you.

This is completely effective when done properly, but most people do it so poorly that it is worse than just chasing her in the first place.

As an example, let's say you wanted to ask a girl on a date. A typical guy might say, "Could I take you out to dinner some time?"

This is an awful thing to say because it implies that spending time with her is some great privilege, which indicates that you are not worth her time.

The typical guy who's trying too hard to act like he's being chased might take things to an extreme and say something like, "I know you want to go out with me, so if I can make time on my schedule, we can have dinner some time."

This may sound ridiculous, but I've seen many guys say inane things like this. She knows that you want to go out with her too, so taking it to this extreme is setting yourself up for disaster.

Better is something more subtle, like "Hey, if we're both free this weekend, we should hang out." This shows interest, but the "we're both free" is so casual that it doesn't seem like you're trying to indicate that you're busy. The statement also doesn't show much enthusiasm—in fact it's more like conversation between two friends.

Your attention

Never give a girl too much attention while you're in the earlier stages of dating. It shows too much eagerness and can indicate that you're chasing her.

When she calls, answer only half the time. Take a long time to return her calls. I personally never answer calls if I'm around other people because I think it's rude, so I usually don't answer calls anyway.

Try making a date with her and then cancelling a day in advance. Don't give her a serious excuse but rather just apologize mysteriously, "Hey, I was really looking forward to seeing you tomorrow, but I'm not going to be able to make it. Hopefully we'll be able to reschedule some other time."

See how that not only shows that you have lots going on in your life, but also shows that her attention isn't that important? Maybe you'll reschedule maybe you won't.

She will judge your relative worth based on the relative amount of attention you give her. If you give her ALL of your attention (as most guys with crushes do) then she will think that you like her way too much.

She'll be scared to show any affection to you because she'll wonder if she's leading you on and get worried about how difficult it will be to break up with you when the time comes.

Devote most of your attention to your normal life and treat her as if she's on probation—you're still not sure if she's going to get a permanent place in your life or not.

If you do this she won't have to worry about you getting too invested and she'll be able to enjoy her time with you and allow herself to become attracted.

The key is to show that you're interested, but not concerned. This will invariably cause her to become more interested and concerned.

Your Standards

Let her know that you have high and specific standards. Chances are that if you're interested in her she meets almost all of these standards, but not some of them.

Imagine that a girl told you she wanted to date a guy who was "tall, drove an SUV, liked swimming, and had blue eyes", and you were tall, drove an SUV, liked swimming, but had brown eyes.

You would constantly wonder if you made the cut or not, and would try to emphasize your best features.

I learned this when a girl did it to me by accident. We were already in a relationship, but it still made me feel like I had to chase her. Of course, I didn't.

If you make her feel like you have high standards, and she meets them, she will feel honored to be with you. If she gets the impression that you're willing to date any girl who's willing to date you, she won't want the job.

Refuse to Chase Her

Girls are naturally very good at the game. She will try to make you chase to get her, but you must always refuse.

Any time she makes a request of you that would result in you taking action that looks like chasing, you must refuse to do it, and possibly make a mockery of it.

"Oh, I can't go out with you tonight because my friends want to go out. Do you want to meet us downtown?"

Sounds tempting, but no, you don't want to meet her downtown.

A typical lapdog would follow her around, scampering for every last crumb of attention. But not you.

A perfect answer would be, "Oh, that's perfect. My friends wanted to get together to watch the OC anyway, so we'll just hang out some other time."

Notice the subtleties in that last sentence. I reframe her flaking as a good thing, showing that I was hoping to get out of the date anyway. I refuse to follow her around, so that she realizes that her attention isn't that valuable to me.

Lastly, and most subtle, I say that I'm going to watch the OC. Mostly girls watch the OC, so she will assume that I'm hanging out with another girl. That will make her jealous and you can bet that she won't flake again.

These sorts of subtleties are lost on most men but women analyze everything people say and are much more perceptive. They know that men aren't as perceptive, and will assume that you let these details slip by accident.

At the same time, make sure that you're able to clearly evaluate what constitutes chasing and what doesn't.

Her cancelling plans so that she can hang out with other friends and you still tagging along is chasing. Her asking to meet an hour earlier because she has a dentist appointment is being reasonable.

Tell her about other girls in your life

Is she the only girl you're seeing? Unless you've been dating for a while, she shouldn't be.

You should definitely ask her for advice or tell her funny stories about other girls you're seeing. She will notice that you're well liked by women, feel competition with them, and want to chase you to ensure that she wins.

If you don't believe me, watch one episode of Elimi-date.

Attitude

The world is your playground.

This is one of the truest statements I know. Outside your house there's an almost inconceivable amount of space filled with diversions and people.

In a given day you're confronted with thousands and thousands of choices ranging from the inconsequential to the life changing.

Social norms are often times appropriate, but sometimes they get in the way.

I'd like to encourage you to think of pickup outside of the box. It doesn't have to be the default concoction of you, a loud club, and drunken girls. Some of my most fun and successful pickups have taken place when I was exploring the world. Some examples:

I was shopping at Target when I saw an attractive girl looking at some items on the shelf. I sped up and slammed my cart into hers.

As they hit I yelled, "HEY! Watch where the hell you're going!" She quickly apologized, and then burst into laughter after she realized that she hadn't even been moving her cart when I hit her.

I then examined the items in her cart and made fun of a few of them. I had made a routine errand exciting for her, so she insisted on getting my number.

Another time I was at my favorite supermarket when I saw a hot girl in the frozen foods section. I walked up to her and said, "Hey, can I have a ride?" She was puzzled, but agreed to let me sit on the end of her shopping cart and get pushed around. I told her to tell me what she wanted and that I would grab it—speed shopping.

She couldn't stop laughing as I tried to grab grated cheese while she pushed me past it.

On an airplane I saw a beautiful girl in the line ahead of me. We were flying Southwest, which has unassigned seating.

When it was my turn to get on the plane it was still mostly empty, with plenty of window and aisle seats available. She had taken the window seat in a row that also had someone in the aisle seat.

I walked up to her and said, "Whoa! Did you save this awesome seat just for me? You shouldn't have done that!"

She laughed and joked that she did. I sat down, and talked with her the whole time, getting her number as I left the plane.

In a more elaborate plan to amuse myself, my wing-man and I called each other and split up.

He handed his phone to a beautiful girl leaving the gym.

"It's for you," he said.

I was on the other end, and I just started talking to her like I knew her forever. After five minutes or so I walked over to her friend and handed my phone to her, saying "It's for you."

When they realized that they were talking to each other, they burst into laughter. We later had date where I almost killed her accidentally, but more about that later.

It's easy to turn routine everyday events into really fun experiences. You end up with a story, a more fun life, and a different perspective.

When you meet a girl in a club and do a so-so job of picking her up, you blend in and become hard to distinguish from the other guys she met that night.

If you smash into her cart at the grocery store, she will probably always remember you. I've had girls remember me years after meeting them once.

Out of your league?

When you're beginning pickup, it's easy to assume that certain girls are out of your league. The truth is that the only way a girl is out of your league is if you decide in your mind that she's out of your league.

I am an average looking guy at best. I'm not a celebrity and I'm not rich. Still, when I was in LA I wooed several models—girls who are paid for their beauty. I even once stole a beautiful girl from an A-list actor.

The simple fact is that every girl, whether she's average or stunning, will respond to attractive qualities in a man.

In fact, I've found that it's actually easier to pick up gorgeous girls. They're so used to guys losing their confidence and treating them like goddesses, that when you stay confident and treat them like normal people, they will respond very strongly to it.

Less attractive girls are more used to guys being confident around them, so the shock value is lessened.

They can also gain validation by shooting down a guy who seems too good to be true. If she doesn't think she's going to get with you, then she can reject you and tell her friends,

"Oh, this guy was totally hitting on me but I told him I had a boyfriend. Haha!"

This lets her save face, rather than having to say:

"This guy was totally hitting on me. I was really into him, but he didn't like me. I want to eat fudge ice cream and cry."

A very attractive girl, however, gets no validation from rejecting guys. She knows that she can get any guy she wants, so she gets more validation from selecting a great guy. Be that guy.

One night I was out picking up with Mystery. I sat with an average looking girl for about half an hour. We exchanged numbers and Mystery and I moved on to another club down the street. As we walked he asked if I was going to call her.

"No."

"Why not?"

"She's not that hot. I always get these numbers from girls I'm not attracted to, and I end up never calling them."

"So why don't you only approach hot girls?"

It was the elusive obvious. Somehow it never occurred to me that I should only be approaching girls I was attracted to. After that I began to approach the hottest girls in the club, and my success rate skyrocketed.

I learned that not only was I in their league, but that it was more fun because I was actually excited about doing it.

A good rule of thumb is to approach the hottest girl in the club first, then the next hottest, and on down the ladder. This way you'll always be approaching the most attractive girls, but you won't have the cop out excuse of "there weren't any 10s at the club, so I didn't approach."

Willingness to leave

This section will surely draw criticism for being "unromantic". That's ok, because it's necessary.

Always be willing to leave. Always.

If you're talking to a girl, be willing to lose her attention. If you've gone on one date, be ready to never see her again. If you're in a relationship, be ready to break up at any time.

The one possible exception is marriage, which is an institution I have no experience with, and thus can't offer any useful insight into. My educated guess, though, would be that you should be ready to divorce.

Pay attention to my choice of words. You don't have to be eager to leave, just willing if the circumstances justify it. If she grows to disrespect you and act in a way that isn't acceptable to you, it's time to jet.

When you see a guy who has given up his willingness to leave he's in trouble.

I've seen so many men who are treated like dirt by their girlfriends, but they stay in the relationship. They're willing to compromise their standards and dignity to hold on to a bad relationship.

When I'm with a girl, she knows that I could break up with her at any point and return to my normal state of overall exuberance quickly. This makes her realize that if our relationship is valuable to her, then she has to treat me with respect and affection.

If she decides to play too many rounds of the "let's see what I can get away with game", she'll find herself single in a heartbeat.

I'd never suggest that you flaunt your power, though. As they say, with great power comes great responsibility. Never threaten to break up and hold it over her head. Just tell her what your standards for being and staying in a relationship are.

And make sure you're really willing and not just acting willing. If you say that you aren't going to be with a girl who cheats, and then she cheats, you must leave her.

If you don't, then she will never take you seriously or respect you.

Katya was a prime example. When we first started dating, I told her that I wouldn't consider having a serious relationship with someone who drank regularly.

I didn't want to change her, but I also didn't want to violate my standards.

She told me that she was considering quitting anyway, and that it was what she wanted to do. Maybe it was foolish for me to believe that, but I really did like her.

Eventually she started drinking again and it got the point where I resented her for it. I had to leave her.

When I broke up with her I really loved her. I drove her to the airport and watched her until she was out of sight. I drove home sobbing, but satisfied that I'd made the right move. Leaving was hard, but I was willing to do it.

If you want to be respected, then prove that you respect yourself first by sticking to your principles at all times.

Dealing with Rejection

During your tenure as a pickup artist, you will be confronted with rejection, probably a lot more than you'd like to be.

I remember in my early days I used to go to a place called *Dallas Nightclub*, which was a giant doughnut shaped bar that surrounded a dance floor. My wing and I would walk around the doughnut taking turns opening and getting summarily rejected.

It's part of the game, so get prepared for it.

First, realize that you are not getting rejected. Your approach is getting rejected. Rejection is one of the few times in life that you are getting 100% honest feedback on your pickup technique. She doesn't know you, what you're like, what your hobbies are, or who your friends are.

Her experience with you is counted in seconds or minutes, and probably isn't representative of you as a person. Taking it personally should be impossible.

Learn from your rejection. What caused her to decide that it wasn't worth getting to know you? Was it your body language, your opener, your posture, or simply that she was busy talking with a friend? Evaluating these things honestly will help you in the future.

Approaching a girl is always a win-win situation. You improve your game and either meet a new girl or learn something about your game. She gets the option of meeting a great guy, or if she rejects you she'll still be flattered that you hit on her. When you look at the big picture you realize that nothing bad can come of it.

It's like getting a bucket full of lottery tickets for free. Most of them won't be winners, but if just one is a winner it makes digging through the bucket worth it.

Of course, you will still have approach anxiety. Some people have it all the time, some people have it rarely. There's no good cure other than to talk to three groups of girls in a row. Once you do that, your anxiety will subside to a manageable level for the night, even if those first three groups didn't go well.

So force yourself to do it, knowing that group number four will be much easier.

Talking vs. Doing

There is one sure way to ruin any chance you have with a girl. People do this all the time, especially in friend zone situations.

I'm talking about breaking down and confessing to a girl that you like her.

"I've been wanting to tell you this for a long time. I love you and I've loved you since we first met."

Guys watch movies where things like this work, and so they get this idea in the back of their heads that it must work sometimes.

It's a Hail Mary and it never works.

I think that most guys know that it doesn't ever work, but they get this delusion that they're different. They think about how easy it would be if she just blurted out back, "I love you too!"

All that stress and agony of not knowing what to do would go away.

Never do this. Trust me—back in the day before I learned pickup, I would do this all the time. It never ever works.

"But I don't want to play games."

What we call "playing games" could just as easily be called, "giving girls the experience they want."

Girls want to feel comfortable and they want a natural progression. They need more time to become attracted to you than you need to be attracted to you.

This sudden amorous confession is very jarring and not natural. It also shows a lack of confidence that you can actually attract her properly. Even if she does like you, she will always rebuff your advances as a knee jerk reaction.

Don't tell her you like her. Instead, show her that you like her by properly attracting her.

Storytelling

Storytelling is both the most important skill in pickup and strangely one of the most overlooked.

When I first got into pickup I learned all of the standard routines and used them successfully.

Later I realized that routines weren't successful because of their content, but rather because of a few characteristics they all shared. Over time I devised the "formula" that makes these routines successful.

Soon, I was telling my own stories in the form of routines, and I found that this worked even better than the memorized ones.

Content

First, realize that the content of the story is hardly important at all. I've heard people say, "but I have no good stories!" This is simply not true.

What matters most about your story is the pacing of the story, and what it says about you. You want a story to give an accurate picture of your personality. Specifically, you want the story to express things that wouldn't be appropriate to directly articulate.

There's no occasion where it would be a good idea to say "I'm brave," but there are a lot of stories you could tell that would lead her to believe that you're brave.

In fact, very few direct statements can be made attesting to your greatness, leaving stories as one of the best ways to express these.

Use this concept to word things very carefully. At first it will take effort, but soon you'll find that it becomes second nature.

I'm not sure that I'm capable of telling a story anymore that doesn't make me shine.

Here's a recent story which happened in my life that I like to tell.

"The other day I was at pitch and putt. That's like golf for people like me who suck at golfing. Anyway, we went to rent our clubs, and I noticed that on the counter there was a bad check that the owners had posted. I thought, 'it's so cool that we can just shame people like that. It's sorta barbaric'.

"As we played golf I wondered if the shaming did any good. I mean—did the guy ever have to deal with the consequences of writing a bad check? I decided to make sure that he did.

"We finished our game of golf, and returned to the counter. After returning our clubs, I looked at the check and wrote down the guy's address and told the lady that I was going to go get her money for her.

"I left the golf course and drove to the guy's house to confront him…"

That seems like a fairly innocuous story, but it's actually loaded with good things about me. First I say that I'm bad at golf. Saying this right off the bat lets her know that I don't take myself too seriously and that I'm not trying to impress her. After all, who would impress someone by saying that he's bad at something?

Next, I show that I'm curious by telling her that I thought about the bad check.

I then show that I'm a generous guy because I tell the lady I'm going to collect her money for her.

Lastly, when I say that I'm going to go confront this guy without even knowing what he's like, she'll get the impression that I'm confident, brave, and fearless. If she later comments on those qualities, I'll likely downplay them.

Girls know that actions speak louder than words. My actions have proved that I'm brave, so saying I'm not will only make me seem modest.

Notice also that you really want to hear what happens next in the story. Every story is a simple arc... it starts off with setting the scene and then quickly builds tension. I will never reveal the punch line of the story until I've built enough tension. The easiest way to build tension is to dwell on the moment before action takes place.

When I tell this story to girls I build up the drive over to the guy's house, how I felt, walking up his stairs, knocking on the door, and waiting for him to answer.

Practice doing this and you'll be able to pick up the cues in the girl's expression to see how committed she is to hearing the punch line.

In general, you want to keep the facts of the story as simple as possible. If you go on a tangent, that tangent had better have an arc just like your whole story. There's nothing worse than a story starting, and then the storyteller says, "And then Bill and I got in the jeep. Bill is my friend who I met in high school, and he was in my chemistry class...."

You will totally lose your listener in your tangent about Bill, and they will assume that since your tangent about Bill is boring, the rest of your story will be boring as well.

On the other hand, feel free to add as many thoughts, emotions, and feelings to the story. These don't confuse the listener, but they do enhance the experience of the story.

When your story peaks and you reveal the punch line, end the story as quickly as possible. With no tension remaining in the story, it's better to leave her wanting more. If she wants to hear more, she'll ask questions.

If she doesn't seem interested in the story at the beginning, try building the tension early. If that doesn't work, just cut off the story, ask a question to regain her interest, and then launch into a new story. ("Wait… have you ever been to Panama? No? Well, if you go, you need to go to this little beach…").

There's nothing worse in a conversation than someone droning on about some story that you don't care about. Be polite and cut off boring stories. Of course you'll probably find that your most interesting stories are well received by any audience.

It's also important to remember that if she or someone else interrupts your story to NEVER resume telling it. It doesn't matter if you think it's the most interesting story in the world. If she doesn't ask for you to continue the story, then drop it. As you become a better storyteller, you'll find that any story you're telling will be so interesting that people will want to hear it to the end.

After the first version of this book was released, several people requested that I include more stories. Here are two of my personal stories that you may find useful in terms of understanding the structure of a story.

They're both longer stories that I might tell while we're sitting on a couch or riding in a car.

The Swimming Pool

Have you ever heard about a site called *PenguinWarehouse.com*? My friend showed it to me a while back because they sell penguins, and my friend figured I might want one.

Of course I did want one, so I spent hours at the site. I researched all of the different breeds and picked the cutest smallest breed, a Snares Island Penguin.

They had a two year old that sounded really cute, so I e-mailed them and told them I'd buy it.

Of course I got REALLY excited getting a penguin and I even named him Magellan.

A few days later I was at Costco with some friends buying stuff for smoothies, when I saw this GIANT swimming pool for sale.

It was one of those above ground ones that rednecks put in their backyards. I thought that it would be perfect for Magellan, so I bought the biggest one they had. It was 3100 gallons and even had a ladder and pump.

We stuffed it into my car and drove back to my house. I decided that I should put it inside because I'd want to be able to hang out with Magellan all the time and it might get too cold for him outside in the winter.

All of my friends told me that it would be a terrible idea to put it inside. I called my dad because he's a home inspector, and he said,

"Look, Tynan. I know you always have these crazy ideas and I always tell you not to do them, but you do them anyway. Trust me on this one—it's a bad idea."

I'm very stubborn, though, and I had already bought the pool, so I decided to just do it anyway.

We unrolled the pool onto my carpet. It filled up the entire living room and barely touched two walls. We inflated the top part and then I got the hose from outside.

It's a really strange feeling holding the hose at full blast when you're standing in your living room.

We sat on the couch and watched it fill for hours. It took so long that we had to stop for the night and restart the next day.

Finally after 12 solid hours it was full.

Then I got an e-mail back from a friend who I'd told about the penguin, and she told me that the site was obviously a hoax.

I told her it wasn't, but after visiting the site again for about five seconds I could tell that it wasn't real. I was just so excited the first time that I wasn't paying enough attention.

So I never got my penguin. BUT... my cute little sister bought me a big plastic one the next Christmas and we named it Magellan.

Lost in Mexico

I love going on cruises. My favorite part about them is just getting away from phone calls and e-mails and everything else.

My friend Jonah comes on the cruises with me sometimes. We both love being on the ship, eating, playing cards, and reading, so getting off at the ports isn't all that important to us.

One time we were somewhere in Mexico. We woke up around 3p.m.. The ship was docked and was leaving again at 5:30p.m..

We went and had some breakfast. After breakfast we told the friends we were eating with that we were going to go walk around Mexico for a few minutes to get some fresh air and sun.

They laughed at us, which was really confusing at the time.

We got off the ship, and there was a HUGE line of people waiting to get back on. The weather was perfect, so I couldn't figure out why they were in such a rush to get back on the ship.

We walked down the pier and got to the sidewalk that ran along the beach. We walked for about twenty minutes down one way, and then decided to head back so that we'd have plenty of time to get on the ship.

We got back to the pier and showed our ship ID cards to the guard at the end of the pier.

"You'd better hurry."

Why? We still had thirty minutes before the ship left.

We started walking up the pier.

"No. RUN!"

We were confused, but we started sprinting. We finally got up to the ship and noticed something strange.

It wasn't on the dock anymore - it was floating in the water and heading out to sea.

I checked my watch. It was only five. We burst out laughing. We'd always wondered what would happen if we missed a ship, and now we were about to find out.

All of the workers on the pier were laughing too.

We got back to the security guard and asked him what we should do. He said to follow him.

The next thing I know he's arranged for us to hire a tiny little speedboat to get us out to the ship, which is now going further and further out to sea.

We sped up to the ship and saw everyone lined up on the railings watching us and cheering. They opened up a hatch in the middle of the ship and dropped a rope ladder.

The little boat pulled up alongside the ship and we actually had to climb twenty feet up the rope ladder to get into the ship.

Then we realized that we forgot to change our watches for the new time zone.

Baiting

Another way to make girls more interested in your stories is to bait them subtly. Tell a boring story that begs a question which will result in a more exciting story.

I once bought a 40 foot school bus with my friends and traveled around the US in it. I really like telling that story, but it never comes up in polite conversation.

Instead I'll wait until she's talking about Vegas or somewhere like that and say something like, "Oh, when my friends and I had a school bus we went there too." It's impossible at that point for her not to ask about the school bus.

If she doesn't take the bait, I drop it.

Practice telling your stories to everyone, and telling boring every day occurrences as interesting stories.

When I got back from Hollywood I was eager to show off my skills to my Austin friends. For fun I decided to tell the most boring stories I could to a girl, and make them as interesting as possible.

I told her about how I clean my room, about how I made dinner for my friends, and about going grocery shopping. I could see her eyes light up with delight because of how I structured my stories, and the next day she told a mutual friend about how interesting I was.

Another useful resource for me has been starting a blog. I write on *www.betterthanyourboyfriend.com* all the time, and it's helped me become a better storyteller.

While I don't memorize routines anymore, I do tend to tell the same stories over and over again, so each time I tell it I switch a few things up to entertain myself and to see how different things work.

A good exercise is to write the letters A-Z on a piece of paper and write a story for each letter. For example:

A – Astral projecting weird roommate

B – Bus

C – Cave exploring

Any time you're looking for a good story, just think about the alphabet and you'll surely remember one of your stories. If you can't come up with a good segue, you can always just tell girls that you're going to tell them a story.

The other day I sat with two random girls and a guy at a restaurant while I waited for my order.

My food arrived at my table, so I said "I'm going to leave and eat, but first I'll tell you a story," and I launched into a story. The next day one of the girls called and told me how much she loved that I told them a story.

Teasing

Several years ago a pickup artist named David DeAngelo popularized teasing girls through a concept called "cocky funny".

This is a very powerful technique, but unfortunately it isn't well understood and is one of the most frequently misused approaches.

In fact, almost every negative depiction of a pickup artist that I've encountered, in the media or by word of mouth, has been someone who attempts to tease but fails.

Some examples of good teasing:

1. "Whoa... you look like some weird sort of stalker girl. Am I going to regret meeting you?"

2. "What? Did you say that you're going to cook your dog? I knew you were a weirdo."

3. "I wouldn't trust you for a second. I'd tell you one of my secrets and then as soon as I leave the club there'd be strangers huddled outside pointing and whispering about me."

4. "Oh my god. You're one of THOSE girls?"

5. "Guess your job? Let's see... judging just from your look, I'd have to say construction worker."

Teasing girls works because it's playful and fun, and simultaneously challenging to the girl. In a fun way she's jokingly being put down, BUT she's always offered a chance to redeem herself.

This is vitally important. You never want something you say to back a girl into a corner. There must always be an obvious answer that she can give that will boost her self esteem back up.

Here are some easy replies to the examples:

1. "No! I'm not a stalker! I only did that once. But I did have this creepy guy stalk ME once..."

2. "I said I'm going to WALK my dog, not cook it! I'm not weird, I promise!"

3. "I'm SO trustworthy. I never tell anyone anything, I promise. And if you see people pointing and whispering, it's probably about your hat."

4. "No, I'm totally not! Just last week I...."

5. "Hahaha... no, I'm a receptionist."

When she responds like this, drop it and agree with her.

"Oh good, I was worried for a second."

If you continue the line of teasing, she will grow tired of it soon and it will seem like you're trying to play games.

Teasing is a form of challenging, not a form of insulting. There's a huge difference here which many people fail to grasp.

Equally important is that you smile, laugh, and keep the atmosphere fun. I've seen people misuse teasing and sincerely insult girls. This leaves the girl offended and you lonely. Not good.

Here are some "teases" I've seen people bomb with:

"What's up with your shirt? That's so out of style."

This is a serious insult. Girls take their clothes very seriously, and you are passing judgement. What can she possibly say to this that would continue the conversation in a fun way?

Her two options are to either get offended and leave, or apologize. "Oh, I know. I don't really like this shirt..."

Neither one is good.

"I don't think you could roll with my friends. We usually go to cooler places than this and I don't know if you're enough of a VIP."

Things like this seem like a challenge, but they're really just insulting and transparent. Girls are able to size up exactly how "cool" you are in a second.

If it's true, then you look like an idiot for rubbing it in. If it's not true, then you look like an idiot for faking.

Here are the types of reactions you want to elicit:

- Laughter
- Amused surprise - "NO! I didn't say THAT!"
- A playful punch or push
- Eager defense - "Oh no, I'm not like that at ALL"

To get the last one, accuse her of being something you know she's not. If she's drinking water, say something like, "Whatever... I can't hang around with alcoholic bar girls like you."

Just make sure it's actually water.

If she dishes it back at you, then that's great. Teasing is a form of affection, and she knows it.

Make sure that you react in a fun playful manner back. When you get defensive from teasing, it shows a real lack of self esteem and makes you seem like you're not a fun guy to be around.

At the same time, realize that there's the same double standard here that exists with other areas of flirting as well. You must try to do everything "right", but when she does something wrong, you have to act as if it was right.

If she teases you and it really is insulting, it's best to laugh it off and not let it affect you. Remember that if she's trying to tease you, she's probably interested.

Once you're with a girl, you want to make teasing much more occasional. Don't tease her in front of your friends. She wants to feel like she's special to you and that you tell your friends good things about her.

If you tease her in front of your friends she might feel as though you're embarrassed to admit that you like her in front of them. I personally have made this mistake.

Dates

Going on a traditional date is one of the worst mistakes you can make.

Dates have become nothing more than contests for men to win a woman's affection. The mere action of taking a woman on a date is admitting that you don't believe that you are worthy to have her.

Any time I meet a woman, I make it clear off the bat that I don't date. Dates are awkward, make people nervous, and put unnecessary pressure on both of you.

Once you start telling girls that you don't date, you'll be amazed to see how many girls will be thrilled with your outlook and more eager to spend time with you.

So what's a good first date substitute?

My personal favorite is the grocery store. If you have a fancy grocery store like Central Market, Trader Joe's, or Whole Foods, this is even better.

When you call the girl, tell her to meet you at the grocery store. She will probably assume that you're planning on buying food to cook her dinner.

She's wrong—you're just getting groceries.

I love to sharply contrast my way of doing things with traditional dating. Every girl is fed up with dating, so these shocking moments will make you look really good.

If possible, get there a few minutes early and begin shopping.

When she sees that you haven't waited for her, she'll
realize that this isn't a "date" where she can screen you,
but it's an opportunity for you to screen her without going too far out of your way.

Your time is valuable, so you're double booking.

I love food, and as someone who's really into health
and nutrition, I have a lot to say about things in the grocery store. Instead of lame questions about her job and
her family, she gets to hear me talk about something I'm
passionate about—food.

You're probably passionate about food, too. When you
pass the fish counter, tell her about that time you went
fishing and ate the fish you caught (I like to talk about
how my little cousins caught a crab at a beach once and
ate it).

When you walk by the bread aisle, talk about that
amazing French bread you ate in France. In fact, next time
you're in the grocery store alone, walk around and think
about stories you could tell that would be prompted by
what you see. You'll be surprised to find the associations
you have with food.

Now here's the best part—after you checkout you're
left in a strange position.

You have perishable foods, so you have to go home.
If you don't like her anymore, simply say, "Hey... it was
really great to hang out with you. I need to go home and
put my food away, but maybe we'll hang out some other
time."

It's a perfect excuse to leave.

If you do like her, then you tell her that you have to
bring your food home. Give her the choice of coming with
you or meeting up with you afterwards. By then she will
most likely feel comfortable coming home with you. If
you've chosen a supermarket near you, then you can say

"Hey, I live a few blocks away, and I have to drop my food off before we go hang out. Want to tag along?"

It's also good to admit that you take girls to the grocery store frequently because it provides a convenient excuse to get rid of them if they are annoying. Girls like to know that you are selective and that they're doing well.

Who should pay?

You should never pay for a first date. Many people feel uncomfortable not paying, and thus wimp out and pay for the date. This is a huge mistake.

You are a prize—a fantastic guy to date, so do you really need to bribe the girl to spend time with you?

Once you're dating her it's fine to pay, as long as she's paying sometimes too. Another good option is to do something that doesn't cost money, like my previous examples. If you really want to do something that costs money (a show, for example), it's not a bad idea to buy the tickets and then tell her that you got them for free.

The key is not to give the impression that you think you have to pay for her attention.If you're doing something very cheap, like getting a cup of coffee, it's ok to pay if it's convenient, but don't go out of your way to do it.

Unique Dates

I don't really see much value in planning a unique date for each girl. I think it's best to just pick one, perfect it, and stick with it. Some people are fickle, though, and won't like the grocery store idea.

Under no circumstances should you do anything that any normal person would ever do. The risk of being categorized as a traditional suitor is too great.

I once found a radio tower that I could climb. A section of the fence was free of barbed wire and there was a ladder running up the middle of the tower. I would tell girls that what we were doing was a surprise, and that she had to wear jeans and sneakers. I'd pick her up, and drive out into the middle of the woods.

By the time we got to the tower, she would usually be slightly scared and entertain the notion that I might be a murderer or rapist. This is actually a good thing because it makes her feel emotion, just like watching a scary movie.

I'd then park the car and tell her that we were going to climb the radio tower. Although one girl had a panic attack and didn't make it to the platform, I never had a girl who refused to climb the tower.

Most loved the idea, especially the romantic view of the city on top. When one girl nearly fell off, I decided that it wasn't worth the risk to keep taking girls up there.

The most important things to remember when choosing a first date are to pick something different, and for it to be something you would do even if she wasn't there.

Bring your friends

Bringing your friends on dates is totally acceptable and will probably help your cause. Again, it's a great way to shock her (don't tell her that your friends are coming), and to show that you disregard dating conventions.

Your friend is also a valuable asset because he knows to ask her, "Hey, has Tynan ever told you about the time he lived with Courtney Love?" That's the kind of topic I could never bring up without looking like I was trying to impress her. If my friend brings it up, he just seems concerned with her entertainment.

Also, your friend knows to excuse himself at the end of the date if things are going well.

After the date, your friend can provide you with valuable feedback on how you did. Just like grocery shopping, when you bring a friend it demonstrates that you aren't putting her on a pedestal; she's just been invited to take part in your everyday life.

Date Ideas

Here are a few date ideas to try. They've all been done with success by either me or my friends. Most are very different from dates she's been on in the past, ensuring that it will always be remembered fondly.

They all provide plenty of time to talk and demonstrate your personality, which is the most important part of the date.

Hike

Take her on a walk through the woods in a local part. Almost every city has "greenbelt" areas where you can walk on trails through the woods.

This is the kind of thing that everyone plans on doing, but people never get around to doing. She'll love the opportunity to actually do it.

If possible, plan it to end up at a creek, lake, or pond and go swimming in your underwear. Tyler from RSD used to ask girls,

"Is your underwear more like a bathing suit or like lingerie?"

Every girl will always say bathing suit and won't feel like she's being slutty when she strips down. Plan accordingly and wear good underwear (incidentally, girls I know prefer boxer briefs, particularly those without flies).

Cooking

Cooking a meal with a girl is a fantastic idea. Go grocery shopping with her and cook together.

Reserve this one for second dates or girls who are already very comfortable with you, since she'll have to come to your house.

If you don't know how to cook, ask her to come over and teach you how.

Shopping

Bring her to shop for something that you already need.

"I'm going to a wedding and need to pick a suit. Help me choose one."

"I just moved into a new apartment and I really need to get some furniture. Girls' apartments always look so good. Come help me get some good furniture."

Make sure that you're going to actually buy what she suggests, though, or she might feel like you've insulted her taste.

Get Married

This is an absolutely hilarious one. Go to a mall and tell her to pretend that she's your fiancée and you need to pick out a ring.

Set a high budget and get the diamond store to show you all the rings.

Girls love weddings, so she'll have a blast the whole time. Tease her by calling her funny names like "sugar cakes" and "pumpkin drop" and being overly affectionate in a playful way.

She'll have to go along with it or risk breaking your farce.

Get Tea

This one is relatively boring, but very easy to get girls to go to.

Make it more fun by challenging her to a game. Claim that you're an expert "Chutes and Ladders" player. Bring the game and play it in the coffee shop.

I did this with one of my recent exes. After the coffee shop closed we moved to a club and set up our scrabble board and played a couple games. We may have been the first people to ever play Scrabble in a club.

She loved that it was so unusual. I killed her in the game and then refused to show her the score at the end, claiming it was a tie.

This is a good move because it shows that you're talented but not insecure. Most guys will insist on beating the girl and making sure she knows it.

Go Skydiving

If you've never gone skydiving, now's probably the time. It's one of the most fun things humans can do, and isn't nearly as scary as it seems.

The amazing rush of endorphines will be unlike anything she's ever experienced. When she reaches the ground she'll be jumping up and down with excitement, and will permanently associate that feeling with you.

Take a Mini Roadtrip

Pick some random destination a few hours away and declare that you're going on a road trip there.

Find the largest ball of twine, a town that shares a name with you, or a random park.

The fun isn't in the destination, but rather being cooped up in a car together for a few hours. Being on a "mission" with a girl and talking to her for hours is very powerful.

Break in Somewhere

One of my friends routinely takes his girlfriends to a botanical garden in Austin.

He only goes at night, when they're closed, and hops the fence. Like some of the other date ideas, this gets adrenaline flowing, but is also very romantic.

I'm not suggesting you do something illegal. I'm just saying that if you do, it will probably be awesome.

Mini Golf

Mini golf is a pretty standard first date, but it can be made more interesting.

Bet something on the outcome of the game.

This can be anything from dinner afterwards to being the other person's personal slave for a day.

If you're going to bet big, make sure you talk a big game that doesn't actually intimidate her.

"You don't want to play against me. I won the 1964 mini golf special olympics in Krakow. I have a perfect record of 2-0."

In something with less chance involved than mini golf, I once bet my car vs. something I can't print in this book. I won.

The Friend Zone

If I were a betting man, I'd wager that there's probably a girl in your life right now who you're interested in who is very interested in only being your friend.

Every guy has been there, but you don't ever have to go there again.

For some reason many people believe that once you're in the friend zone you can't ever get out. My experience has proven to me that the exact opposite is true. Being in the friend zone is actually a head start, if you know what you're doing.

Before I learned that fine art that we call pickup, I was systematically sorted into the friend zone by nearly every girl I met.

Now things are different. I would love for a girl I was interested in to try and slot me as a friend. That small speed bump of a challenge would be a delight to overcome.

Let's examine the problem. She likes you, but doesn't want to sleep with you. You're already half way there! Picking up all of the habits and tips in this book will get you most of the way there, but she'll definitely need a jump start to help her notice that you've changed into a more attractive homo sapien.

The best way to do this is to make her jealous. Sounds mean, but she'll be glad you did it once she has the pleasure of a relationship with you.

The very best option is to meet a new girl and make sure she knows about it.

The next best option is to invent a girl and make sure she doesn't know you invented her. I wouldn't personally do this, since I am a strong proponent of complete honesty, but it's so effective that I feel obligated to include it.

Shock her one day and ask her a sexual question. Maybe you wonder which positions are best for making a girl orgasm. If you haven't before, you've now breached that line between polite and intimate conversation.

She will hardly bat an eye since she's used to talking to girls in much more graphic detail than you could possibly imagine, but it will hurdle you into the coveted grey area.

Now you've got her thinking about you sexually, since her first instinct will be to visualize you with a girl. She'll also wonder who this girl is. If she asks, just tell her that you don't want to talk about it until it's a little more real (Haha! Get it? She won't).

Meanwhile, start hanging out with her less, but make an effort to make the times you do hang out more fun. This should cause her to eagerly anticipate the times you share, and will turn her into the pursuer.

When you're hanging out and talking, make a point to talk about sexual things.

Girls love talking about sex (have you ever seen *Sex and the City*?), and getting a male point of view is fun for them. Occasionally switch from sexual talk to normal talk so that she doesn't think that you're only interested in one thing.

This should go without saying, but don't joke around too much while talking about sex; it may make her feel like you're not comfortable talking about it.

Now you've set the stage for a magnificent exit from that dreaded Friend Zone, so it's time for action.

For this feat, we turn to our best friend, the cuddle.

Cuddling

Cuddling is magical because it straddles the line between platonic intimacy and the kind of intimacy you're after.

In practice it's easy to start on one side of that line and slowly weasel your way to the other side. She's already attracted, and the change is so subtle that it won't ring any alarm bells in her head.

Lie down to watch a movie and set up a pillow on the ground close to the TV with a blanket near it. I used to always do this anyway since I had poor vision.

In Hollywood we had a sea of pillows and movies projected on the ceiling, so it was even more natural. Use whatever excuse you must, but make it so that you are going to lie on the ground near the TV.

Lie down and encourage her to lie with you with your arm around her. This might sound drastic, but it's really a very small deal, and easy to execute casually.

Perfect.

Now you have two hours and you only have to move six inches or so. Your goal is to have her hugging you with your legs intertwined before the movie ends. This can be accomplished by doing things like putting your legs on top of hers as if it's comfortable like that.

Try getting up to go to the bathroom, and then resuming the movie with a slightly closer position. Squirm as if you're uncomfortable, and just happen to end up with your hand touching her stomach.

For some reason if you have a blanket and she can't see what's going on, she will find it much more acceptable and will be more enthusiastic (okay, there's a superb chance she's annoyed that you're taking too long to kiss her and this is all totally unnecessary, but you don't want to mess up the friendship and blow your chance, so take it slow).

Once you're halfway there anyway, turn and look at her. When she looks at you, kiss her. I'll leave it up to you from here, now that you're clear out of the friend zone.

Social Circle

One very common case of escaping the friend zone is dealing with girls who are in your social circle. Maybe you've known her since sixth grade, have always had a crush on her, and have never been seen as anything more than a friend.

Or sometimes a friend of a friend will start hanging out with you and your friends. You didn't have a chance to go through your normal sequence of events, so now you're "just friends" by default.

In situations like these you're effectively competing against all of your other male friends. If she's been in your circle for a while then chances are several of you have crushes on her.

But even if they aren't actively pursuing her, they're still competing because she may be interested in them anyway.

You will be judged by her based on who your friends are and how you interact with them. After all, do you know anyone who isn't very similar to most of his friends?

What you want to do is build up your friends, which should be pretty easy since you like them and know them well. At the same time, you want to be seen as one of the leaders in the group.

That doesn't mean that you should boss your friends around or try to act superior to them. It simply means that you should assume responsibility within your social circle.

Come up with events for everyone to go to. Offer to drive. Suggest restaurants and movies. Call people and coordinate when you're all going to hang out together. Throw parties or barbecues for everyone.

Overall you want her to see you as being a great friend and a leader. Sometimes guys think that the right thing to do is cut down their friends to try to look superior. This looks pathetic and should never be done. You will ruin your chances and she may become interested in someone in the group who treats his friends with more respect.

Begin subtly teasing her while you're hanging out with your friends. Nothing too overt, just the occasional playful shove or friendly banter.

Gradually ramp up the amount of attention and flirting you're directing towards her.

Call her and invite her to do something with you that sounds like a date.

"Hey, it's Tynan. Let's grab some dinner."

See how she reacts. If she seems comfortable then go for it and procede normally. If she seems a bit hesistant, invite some of your other friends along. She'll feel a bit silly for assuming it was a date, but that alone will jump start her mind into thinking about dating you.

Typically at this point she should start chasing you, or at least finding opportunities to be alone with you.

In situations like this it's best to progress slowly because if you make her feel uncomfortable the awkward situation will be magnified by your friends. Rumors will spread and everyone will wonder how to act around you two.

When I was in high school I had a huge crush on a girl. I confessed this out of nowhere and told her, which obviously caused her to recoil. Things were very strained between us for a long time.

You can't imagine how awkward it was when we were playing spin the bottle and it was time for me to kiss her. You could have heard a pin drop as all of my friends waited to see what would happen.

If she doesn't chase you immediately, spend a lot of time alone around her but move slowly. She's not going anywhere, so there's no harm in taking a few weeks.

Sometimes people assume that since she's a friend, standard indicators that she likes you don't apply.

"Yeah, she likes to cuddle with me on the couch, but that's because she's my friend."

Don't think like this. If she's doing things that indicate that she's attracted to you, then she's attracted. That doesn't mean to blurt out "I LIKE YOU!", but I does mean that things are going well.

As a guideline, if she's spending a good amount of time around you without your other friends, she's probably hoping you're going to make a move.

Choose Your Own Relationship

The notion of one guy, one girl, a few years of dating, a wedding, and a few kids is the American standard for a relationship. As a result, most people end up in that sort of configuration by default.

Sure you may only get a few steps down the path (hopefully past the first!), but it's still a specific path that you're on.

Is it right for you?

Well, it's the overwhelming popular favorite, so it's probably a pretty good choice, but that doesn't mean that it's necessaryli for you.

Think about what you want. Do you want a girlfriend? Do you want friends with benefits? Maybe you're looking for a wife to settle down with. Perhaps you just want a one night stand. Maybe you're like me and you think it would be awesome to have a three way relationship. You could be hoping for another dude to join you—I don't know.

Whatever it is you want, make sure that your actions reflect your goal. If you're looking for a three way relationship, you probably don't want to meet girls in church, unless you're a Mormon.

If you're looking for a girlfriend, maybe you should frequent book stores and restaurants you love.

If you are looking for a wife, you probably have no business being in a club. There are always exceptions, but why not maximize your chances of success?

I think a club is great for practice, but once I put in enough time to gain proficiency, I stopped going to clubs. I don't like them, and most girls that I would be interested don't spend a lot of time at them.

This decision actually became clear to me when I decided to talk to 100 groups of girls in a month. It was an arbitrary challenge that a friend and I had made for other people, so we figured we ought to try it ourselves. In that month I succeeded in talking to 100 groups of girls, but in the end I didn't find a single one I really liked!

What a waste of time.

After that I swore off clubs, except for Wednesday night when I hosted Karaoke.

Lay your goals on the table with girls that you meet. If they know what you're looking for, they'll probably try to adapt to fit that role if they're flexible.

If they're looking for the same thing that you're looking for, perfect. If not, then you've just saved some time and you can talk to the next girl.

Phone Game

The phone is an important stage in pickup, and deserves its due attention.

Many people like to get e-mail addresses or text phone numbers, but I would argue that there's no substitute for a good old fashioned phone call—especially if it's done right.

Your timing and intonation are two valuable tools, and your voice is a powerful anchor. Why let those things go to waste?

When should you call?

This is a highly debated and entirely unimportant consideration.

The bottom line is that you should call whenever you want. I've seen Mystery call girls the same night many times, and I've called girls a month later because I forgot to call.

It really doesn't matter nearly as much as what you say and how you say it.

I usually just call the girl the next day. If you've done things right she likes you and is looking forward to your call anyway.

Getting her phone number

When I first got into the game in Austin, getting girls to call back was easy.

One call, one message, and they would call back.

Then when I got to Hollywood I discovered that it was basically impossible to get girls to return calls. As a result I decided that it was important to have girls ask for MY number instead.

Since making that decision, I have made nearly every girl ask for my number. I like to push the interaction as much as possible, but the phone number is a testing point, indicating whether or not you've done a good job.

If you have done a good job, she will definitely ask for your number. No interested girl is going to let you leave without giving it up. If you haven't fully attracted her, she won't ask for your number, but she wouldn't have answered your call anyway.

When the time comes for you to part ways, say "Well… I have to go. It was really nice meeting you, and it's a shame we'll never see each other again."

Make sure she knows that you're ready to leave, by taking a half step away. Inevitably she will reply and say something to the effect of, "Why not?"

Tell her that you don't go out often, but that you never know. If you've told the "100% Perfect Girl Story" to her, then this will have particular impact.

She will almost certainly ask if you want her number.

Laugh as if it's a joke and say, "Haha… no. I like you a lot, but I always get numbers at clubs and never call them back."

This is a truism for girls that doesn't really apply to guys. She won't realize that, and will just assume that you're popular. She will also relate to it, and will usually laugh when she realizes that she does the same thing.

Continue back and forth with the objections. The hotter she is the more you'll need, especially if you're in a high pressure environment like a club.

Other valuable objections are:

"No, you're drunk so you'll totally forget who I am."

"I don't have my phone." (even if you do)

Eventually say, "Well, I'll tell you what. I'll give you my number and you can call me, although I totally think you're drunk and you'll forget."

Once a girl decides that she wants your number, she will not give up, so feel free to make this as difficult as possible. She will also remember that you took effort to get, and will rationalize that you're worth it. After she gets your number, get hers so that you'll "know who's calling".

This little dance will maximize the chances of her calling, but will leave you with her number in case she forgets.

Never settle for an e-mail or a business card. Turning down either of these items is a powerful gesture, and will increase your chances at getting a number.

"No… I don't want your e-mail address, you dork."

Asking for an e-mail address instead of a phone number seems easier, but will be more difficult in the long run, and it's obvious that you didn't have the nerve to go for the phone number.

The First Phone Call

The first phone call is the most important, but it's also very easy. Call her number, and if she doesn't answer, call back immediately.

Tyler from Real Social Dynamics discovered that this is an amazing technique to get her to answer. Most people, especially popular girls, won't answer a call if they don't know the number. For some reason, this avoids that trap.

If she doesn't answer on the second call, leave a message.

If she was screening because she didn't know that it was you, this could result in a call back. It's best to have a story ready to tell her.

As soon as she answers say, "Hey, this is Tynan. Guess what happened to me today?"

This is how friends talk on the phone (which you should know, if you have friends), so acting in this way will make her feel more comfortable with you. After your story, continue to chat with her for a little while and then abruptly say, "well, it was cool talking with you. I've got to go meet my friends."

Do not invite her to anything.

If you put in one phone call like this, you can be sure that she'll answer the next time you call, and until then she'll be wondering why you didn't ask her out.

Girls love anticipation, so give it to them!

Other phone calls

After the first phone call it's okay to ask her out after you've chatted for a few minutes. Don't be too eager.

The best way to get her to go somewhere with you is to make spur of the moment plans. If she commits to doing something NOW, there's a low chance of flaking. If you plan for next week she has time to talk herself out of it or "get a better offer".

Doing this also makes it seem like less of a date, which is good for many reasons. If she objects, feel free to convince her to go, but not in a needy way.

Don't say things like:

"But I REALLY want to see you!"

"Come on... don't you want to hang out with me?"

"Well, why did you give me your number, then?"

Instead, say things like:

"Are you kidding me? You'd rather stay home and do laundry than go grocery shopping?"

"Oh… are you one of those weird hermit people?"

"Don't be shy. Everyone's doing it."

In general you want to phrase your convincing arguments to infer that there's something wrong with HER for not going, not something wrong with YOU.

After all, you're the most fun guy in the world to hang out with, right?

It's also okay to bully her in a funny way. For example:

"I'm about to go grocery shopping… want to come along and help me check the produce?"

"Sorry, not tonight…"

"Ok, great. I'm going to leave in 5 minutes so you should leave now and I'll meet you there."

"Haha… no, I said I can't go."

"Perfect… just meet me by the bananas."

Often times you'll get her laughing enough that she'll think that it will be fun to hang out with you.

If she has other plans, tell her to cancel them. If she has a date, ask if you can come along to chaperone. I'm just dying for a girl to say yes to that some day.

The general idea is that if she isn't going to come out with you that night, you want to show her that you're a fun guy and that she's missing out, without actually saying anything like that.

Ongoing Calls

Once you're going out with the girl you'll probably have frequent contact with her over the phone and over text messaging, and won't always be asking her to do something.

Just remember that if you're doing things right, the more time you spend talking to her or around her, the more she's going to like you. This is the main benefit of a personality and lifestyle driven approach over a purely routine based approach where it's possible to run out of material.

There are a few basic rules you need to follow to make sure that your phone calls and texts are working for you and not against you.

After the first two calls or so, never call her or text her more than she calls you. Girls subconsciously pick up on this eagerness and will be less interested in you.

Call her almost every time she calls you. Don't always answer. My rule of thumb (for everyone unless I'm expecting an important call) is to only answer the phone when no one else is around.

I think it's a bit rude to take calls in front of other people. As a result, most times that girls call me, their calls go to voicemail.

Always try to be the first one to hang up. I don't mean that you need to race to hang up, but rather that you should end the conversation before she's sick of talking with you.

"I guess I should go be productive now. Awesome talking with you, of course, and I'll see you in a couple hours."

Relationships

Maintaining a good relationship is easy if you start off on the right foot. The tone you set in the very beginning will hold through for the whole relationship and will be the easiest tone to maintain.

One of the main reasons I stress the importance of building yourself into a person who is genuinely attractive, interesting, and memorable is because that's the type of person who girls want to stay with on a long term basis.

This is a good thing even if you aren't going for a traditional relationship. Because I operate this way, I can go years without seeing or talking to a girl, but when I'm in her city she's glad to see me.

Instead of thinking about "getting a girl into a relationship", focus on making yourself so compelling that she will always want to be around you.

Honesty

You can attract and sleep with girls by lying, but it would be nearly impossible to maintain a relationship that started off this way. Instead I suggest complete honesty from the beginning in every aspect of your relationship.

Don't offer information that might offend her, but do answer questions honestly even if the response might offend her. Once you are caught lying once, even about something minor and innocuous like when you last saw your ex-girlfriend, you will never be fully trusted again.

If you're honest about everything, even the bad, you will ALWAYS be trusted. You're not expected to be perfect, so don't worry if she doesn't like the truth once in a while.

Respect

In Canada there is a scientific lab called the "Love Lab". They analyzed thousands of relationships and found the single biggest indicator of a relationship that is about to fail is contempt.

Contempt, or resentment, will destroy a relationship faster than anything. If she resents you, she will leave you, cheat, or make you want to leave her. If you resent her you will do the same.

How do you avoid resentment?

Picking the right person will be a large part of it. If you like staying out with your friends until 3am every night and she wants to curl up with you and go to sleep at 10pm every night, that might be a future source of resentment.

If you resent her for something, it's best to take personal responsibility for it if you can. Accept that you like her despite her flaws. Resolve to be at peace with her flaws because they're part of what makes her her.

This isn't always easy, but it's probably the only option.

Always keep your word. This builds respect as well as trust.

Treat her well, but not too well. Never put her on a pedestal or put more effort into the relationship than she's willing to put in. This will cause resentment on her part.

At the same time, let her know that you like her, love her, respect her, and are happy to be with her. Make sure that she knows that you have choices and chose her, and that you aren't with her by default or out of convenience.

Make her work at the relationship too. I always have girls do my laundry, cook for me, and help me with projects. Girls are very nuturing and submissive by nature, so they like being told what to do if (and only if) it is appreciated.

"Baby, thank you so much for doing my laundry. If it wasn't for you I'd be wearing dirty clothes all the time."

"Your food is so amazing. Before we were dating I used to eat black beans and toast every day."

Setting Rules

I would highly recommend never setting any rules for your girlfriend and not accepting any on yourself.

Girls will not follow rules you set for them unless they want to. Unlike men they are very emotional and will often do things based solely on emotion.

Instead, show her respect and tell her that you won't make any rules for her and if she starts acting in a way that's unattractive to you or vise versa, then you can go your separate ways.

In a very short amount of time she will know you very well and will know what's attractive to you and what is offensive enough that you'll be willing to break up with her over it. It's better to treat each other as adults rather than make rules for each other.

If she tries to set rules for you, don't just agree to them and secretly break them. Instead, tell her something like,

"I think you know me well enough to trust me to act in a way that's respectful to you, but I don't think either of us have any business telling the other person what to do."

Arguments

Never get angry with a girl. Never.

Even if she has just cheated on you, you can't get angry at her. If she just smashed your car, you stay calm. Anger is a weak emotion, and she knows it.

You can argue with her as long as you're doing it with the intention of straightening out the disagreement and continuing the relationship.

If you're doing it with the intention to make her feel bad or get back at her, stop. If you can't come to an agreement, you have two options.

1. Suck it up and deal with it. I'd recommend doing this before the argument even begins. Whenever I'm about to confront a girl about something I think, "am I willing to lose her over this?"

If I'm not, I suck it up and don't say a word. This helps put things in perspective as well.

Girls want to hear about your feelings. Share them, but don't ever express discontent with something you're not willing to break up with them over if they don't fix it.

Instead, focus on praising them for things you like that they do.

2. Tell her that you think it's better to stop seeing each other. This forces her to decide whether or not she's willing to back down to keep the relationship.

I'm not in any way suggesting that you use this method to manipulate your girlfriend. If she isn't willing to back down, you have no option but to break up.

I had a girlfriend who wanted more attention from me during a time that I was very busy. I loved her but had to stick to my priorities and work. Here's what I said:

"Baby, you know I love you and love spending time with you, but right now it's critically important to my life that I get this work done. I can, and would like to, make time to see you twice a week, but right now that's all the time I have. If that's not enough for you then I completely understand, and we can break up."

This avoids all of the bickering, name calling, and arguing in circles that most couples have during their disagreements. It makes her realize what's at stake and gives her the power to choose what will be best for her.

In my case she chose to keet seeing me and never complained about not having much time with me. In fact, because the issue was totally resolved it didn't bother her anymore and our relationship was great.

This may seem like a very extreme way of resolving arguments, but they're very effective. This method completely eliminates drama and contempt for the other person.

Most traditional arguments get very emotional and leave both people offended and the relationship worse off.

Neediness

I feel like I've probably covered this sufficiently in this book, but I don't mind reiterating some of the key points because this is the number one killer of relationships.

I'm talking, of course, about neediness.

Neediness manifests itself when you derive your self esteem or self worth from your girlfriend. If she likes you then you feel like a great person and you're proud. If she's slipping away you feel unattractive and worthless.

The tangible signs of neediness are things like:
- Calling her too much
- Asking her about how much she likes you
- Asking her about the relationship

- Insisting on spending all your time with her
- Trying to restrict her from hanging out with other friends (male or female)

If you EVER catch yourself doing any of these things, STOP and do the exact opposite. If you call her too much, don't call her until she calls you again, even if it takes days.

If you were getting jealous (even subtly) of her hanging out with her friends, say something like,

"Hey, I've got some work to do tonight, why don't you hang out with Todd and Anissa?"

This is critically important. If you're a needy guy you will get total disrespect from your girlfriend. She'll talk to her friends and say things like,

"Oh, Steve? Yeah, he does whatever I want and follows me around like a puppy dog."

Having a life

One very common error is when a guy gets into a relationship with a girl and she becomes his entire world. He stops hanging out with his friends, his hobbies get sidelined for hers, and all of his attention and thoughts are with her.

Besides being a ridiculous way to live this is very unattractive to her.

She started dating you initially because you had an interesting life and an interesting personality. When you get sucked into her world you have no value left to offer. She's already an expert there.

Do make friends with her friends, get involved with her interests, and pay attention to her. But, make sure that she's becoming equally, or more, invested in you.

And besides, your friends will always be there for you. Who knows how long things will last with her?

Special Considerations

We've covered all of our bases now and you should have a good idea about what is and isn't attractive to women. Before I leave you, I'd like to touch on a few last special situations that you might find yourself in.

Her Friends

I hope that this doesn't apply to you and that you find my advice completely unnecessary. Only recently have I discovered that many men don't like meeting their girl's friends.

This is such a stupid preference that it's difficult for me to even know where to begin.

Girls are intensely social creatures. Think of how analytical men are—that's how social women are. Their friends' opinions of you will largely dictate how they feel about you. You should absolutely jump at any opportunity to meet her friends and to win them over.

The techniques I've outlined in this book will make you well liked by man, women, and beast alike. If her friends are raving about you then her opinion of you will rise. If they don't like you, then you're doing something wrong anyway; the friends are the least of your problems.

Take the opportunity to talk about the girl with her friends. They'll be happy to share funny stories, insights into her personality, and other pickup gems.

Jealousy and Cheating

Jealousy is one of the least attractive traits a man can have. It doesn't matter how justified it is—it will still sink your ship every time.

I remember one girl who was sleeping with a friend of mine even though she had a boyfriend. When I'd hang out with her she would complain about how her boyfriend was always so jealous of other guys.

Read that again—she's complaining that her boyfriend suspected something that was absolutely true! He had every right to be jealous.

The only solution to the jealousy problem is to show no jealousy whatsoever. It doesn't matter if she's flirting with every guy she knows and whispering sweet nothings into their ears. You need to act as if it couldn't concern you less.

The fact is that if she wants to flirt with other guys – or do more than just flirt, there is no way you're going to stop her.

If she's reasonably attractive then she has a line of guys just waiting for her attention. If she's unreasonably hot, then you can bet that she has armies of men fawning over her constantly.

Your petty jealousy will serve as no deterrent to her doing whatever she pleases.

It's a very common occurrence for a girl to be faithful to her boyfriend, but then he gets jealous and possessive, imagining that she's sleeping around. He expresses his jealousy, which then leads her to think, "If he thinks I'm sleeping with other people, I may as well just do it."

This sounds crazy, but I've heard girls say that VER-BATIM.

It's important to give a girl all the freedom she wants. Show her that you trust her, and she will want to earn your trust. You probably have female friends that you're not sleeping with, so extend her the same courtesy. If she wants to go out with her guy friends, don't protest.

I actually encourage girls to do things like this because I think it ultimately makes them happier in the relationship.

After training yourself not to be jealous for a while, you will actually not feel jealous anymore. Being 100% jealousy free makes you that much more appealing to women and it makes your relationship less stressful.

One last word of advice: if she's cheated before, she'll do it again. Maybe not with you, but be prepared for the possibility and accept it up front. If she's faithful then consider yourself lucky.

Last Minute Resistance

Mystery discovered a long time ago that even when girls want to sleep with you, they sometimes have second thoughts at the last minute.

There are a handful of reasons for this, ranging from them wondering if you'll think they're a slut to them following stupid books like *The Rules* and thinking it's not ok to have sex without first completing three proper dates.

I have two fantastic solutions to this problem.

The first is to promise them that you won't have sex with them. I use this one if I can see that she really wants to make out with me or fool around, but is worried that she'll end up having sex, going farther than she's ready for. If this is the case, I simply say,

"Look, I know you're attracted to me and I'm attracted to you. You're probably worried that we're going to have sex, but I promise you that we won't. In fact, no matter what you do, I give you my word that I won't have sex with you tonight."

Now, no girl has ever heard this before. It's a strange statement and I say it with a straight face backed with sincerity.

Inevitably they say ok and allow themselves to get comfortable and make out with me. In fifteen minutes or so they'll be ready to have sex and will make that clear to you.

What you do from that point on is up to you, but I have always stuck to my word and refused to have sex. I think it's extremely important to always stick to my word, and I know that it will only make her more eager next time.

She'll respect you for keeping your word when it's very difficult to do so, and will rightfully trust you even more in the future.

Sometimes she is ready to sleep with you but has a strange mental hang up that's preventing her from doing it. Often girls promise themselves that they won't sleep with you before coming to your house—I don't know why they do this, but it can offer token resistance.

The best way around this is to point out that they're being weird.

If I found that we were fooling around, but she stopped me at a certain point, I would say, "Why are you acting so weird?"

"What do you mean?"

"Well, it's obvious that we like each other and want to be together, but I can tell that you're playing some sort of mind games with yourself. It seems really strange to me that you would resist what you naturally wanted to do. It just seems weird to me."

Being so candid will make her realize that you understand what's going on in her mind and will almost certainly cause her to realize that she's being ridiculous.

Keep in mind that sometimes girls genuinely aren't ready to sleep with you because you haven't spent enough time getting to know each other yet. This can be a legitimate objection and the remedy is not to pressure her, but rather to spend more time getting to know her.

I personally only use these sorts of techniques when it's obvious that she's artificially stopping herself from doing something she wants to do, and I'd suggest that you do the same.

Girls with Boyfriends

I suppose that this chapter is expected, given my now famous theft of Mystery's girlfriend.

Ironically, none of these tactics were used on Katya. I stole her by accident—Mystery and she weren't getting along very well and she and I had become friends.

When he ignored her, she sought my company, and I had enough other attractive attributes in place that she fell in love with me.

Since that time, although I enjoyed my relationship with Katya, I have decided that it was a mistake to date a friend's ex and would never repeat such a mistake. I've since apologized to Mystery and we're on good terms again.

Even so, I have no moral qualms getting involved with girls who have boyfriends that I don't know.

The truth is that I'm in no place to judge their relationship or to make assumptions. He could be a perfect boyfriend, but it's equally likely that he's a player who sleeps around and this is her way of trading up. Maybe they have an open relationship. Maybe her boyfriend isn't even real.

The choice of fidelity is for the girl to make, not you. Trying to get a girl to cheat is also a test, and a bit of a catch-22. If she cheats then I will not take her seriously and won't have a serious relationship with her. If she breaks up with her boyfriend and then becomes involved with me, I'll have a lot of respect for her.

Never ask if a girl has a boyfriend. If she wants to tell you, then the truth will come out. If she doesn't want to tell you, then don't corner her into an awkward situation.

Often a girl only wants to tell you that she has a boyfriend so that later she can feel like she's absolved from responsibility because you knew that she had a boyfriend.

If her dilemma is that superficial, all it takes a quick acknowledgement and an indication that it's not a big deal to you. Try one of these responses on for size:

"No way! Me too! What a weird coincidence!"

"Hey, don't go dumping all your problems on me."

"Lucky you!"

"He sounds amazing."

"I'll be discreet."

If, by her tone, you can tell that she has a legitimate objection then take the situation a bit more seriously.

You can also base your response on how early in the conversation he came up. If it was soon after you met her a superficial comment will probably suffice. If you've been hanging out for hours and she just came back to your apartment, it's more likely to be a genuine concern.

Your primary goal for a girl with a boyfriend is to get her to argue against him. The best way to do this is to take HIS side on an argument, and argue what a great guy he is.

At the same time, you want to paint him as someone who is insecure, boring, jealous, and underqualified to be with her. Most guys are exactly that, so it's an easy hint to drop.

I discovered this tactic when I was lying in bed with a girl talking about her boyfriend. She would cuddle with me but refused to kiss me.

"I have a boyfriend."

"Really? What's he like?"

"He's really nice. I live with him in Chicago."

"That's awesome... Chicago's a fun town to be in, so it must be cool to get to go out, and then go home to your boyfriend who's waiting for you."

Now, I know that 90% of guys are so insecure that they hate it when their girlfriends go out. I first met her at a club, so I knew that she likes going out.

"Well, sorta," she replied, "He doesn't really like it when I go out."

"Why not? I love it when a girl is independent enough to go have fun without me."

Now I'm painting myself as the opposite of her boyfriend, but I'm acting like I just don't understand how he could feel that way. I'm not commiserating with her, I'm just being curious.

"I know! He's just a little jealous sometimes."

"Oh, you shouldn't be too hard on him. Most guys get jealous, and it's just a sign that he's head over heels for you."

Now I'm saying that most guys are jealous, a negative trait, and implying that I'm one of the few guys who aren't. I then say that it's a sign that he's head over heels for her.

This will almost certainly bring back memories of him pursuing her in an unattractive way.

"Yeah, he is. I try to convince him not to be insecure, but he always is."

"Well, I'm sure he's just a really nice guy. Most guys are insecure, so it's not a bad idea to settle on the one who has the most other good things going on."

No girl wants to be dating a "nice guy" and no girl wants to "settle". It seems like I'm being a good guy and sticking up for her boyfriend, but really I'm pointing out flaws that I'm sure he has, without seeming to have an agenda.

If she brings up a suspicion that he's cheating on her, your work is done. For some reason this happens rather frequently.

"Well, I know that most guys cheat, but just because he spends a lot of time traveling doesn't mean he's not one of the few who doesn't cheat."

It's true, but it allows her to realize what is probably the reality: if she assumes that he's cheating, he probably really is. At this point your work should be done and she will be more attracted than ever.

If you decide to take the more obvious tack and try to convince her that her boyfriend sucks, she'll invariably defend him until it's her moral imperative to remain faithful to him to prove that he's worth it, even if he's really not. Remember that a lot of girls are stuck in dead end relationships just waiting to meet a great guy like you.

Girls don't usually run around single for long, so your best bet is often to steal a girl from the tail end of a dying relationship.

A Case Study

This last story is a field report that I never wrote.

I was so wrapped up in other things at the time that it slipped through the cracks. Most other field reports have been lost in the winding passageways of my brain, but this was a performance so good that I'll probably always remember it.

Some nights we go out in pairs, or alone, but tonight it's a big group. Tyler is here, Mystery's current girlfriend, Katya, is with us, as are a number of other notable pickup artists who don't come into play.

My current peacocking accessory is the venerable feather boa, an accoutrement guaranteed to make even the iciest girl wonder about me.

No one looking at me will assume I'm average, for better or worse.

As I walk into White Lotus, a popular club in the center of Hollywood, I see an amazing girl walk straight towards me. She isn't an 8 and she isn't a 9. She's an undisputed 10 by anyone's standards and she knows it.

She looks me in the eyes, a feeble attempt to make me lose my edge. I stare back.

"What's that thing for?"

She's looking at my boa, trying to see how confident I am.

"It's my pet chicken."

She wasn't expecting that.

"What?"

"I had a pet chicken that I loved. I tried to feed him Goldschlager to make him lay golden eggs, but it didn't work. He died and so I made a boa out of him. Thanks a lot for bringing it up."

"…"

She's speechless. She's waiting for me to laugh, but I have a dead serious look on my face. She can't tell if I'm serious or not.

"Haha!" I burst out laughing, "You actually believed that I had a pet chicken and I tried to make it lay golden eggs?"

I turn around slightly, just so that she knows that I'm willing to leave at any time. She stammers something about knowing that I was lying, but it's too late. I've completely disarmed her and she knows that I'm confident.

Likewise, I know that she's intrigued and that I'll have plenty of opportunities to talk to her later. The effect that an average looking guy like me ending a conversation with a beautiful girl like her has is devastating. She'll have to talk to me later.

We mill about the club talking amongst ourselves and to the masses of single girls in attendance tonight. I point out the girl to Tyler.

"Dude… I was going to talk to her, but I know that even I don't have a chance. If you want to, go ahead, but she'll be impossible."

He's being modest—I've seen him do amazing things that I could never recreate.

She's now sitting at a round table with an older guy who has bought an expensive bottle of champagne. Behind her are her friends, all beautiful girls in their own right. If I didn't have my sights set on her, any one of them would be nearly as appealing.

I walk up to the tables. Immediately one of her friends blurts out, "can I make out with you?"

This doesn't happen often. I now know for a fact that she told them about me. I want to make out with the girl, but it would be a dead end. I would have become a puppet for their entertainment and she would assume my confidence was faked.

"No." I say it with a dismissive tone, as if she just asked me for a million dollars.

Without asking I sit next to the girl so that she's in between me and the older guy.

"I'm Dara," she says.

I introduce myself, but the guy doesn't say anything. He's clearly jealous and thus has already eliminated himself from the competition.

I begin launching into a few stories that happened that week. She listens to every word. A large plate of sushi arrives that the man has ordered. Within a few minutes she's feeding me the sushi with chopsticks. The man looks on with envy, and I silently thank him for illustrating why acting normal is a losing move.

I sit for a while with them and she tells me interesting stories as well. She's a professional model, but is surprisingly smart, especially in Hollywood where smart girls are rarer than unicorns.

I notice my friends nearby. It's a perfect opportunity to show that I'm not putting her on a pedestal and that I still prefer my normal friends. I excuse myself and rejoin my friends.

With a plate of sushi there, I know she's not going anywhere. Just in case, I've let her wear my boa so that she has to see me before she leaves. This is a great tactic developed by Mystery.

Later she finds me again and puts my boa back on my neck.

"Will you buy me a drink?"

"Haha. No."

I have strong convictions, and I'm not about to bend them just because she got lucky in the gene pool.

"Why not?"

"I don't buy drinks for girls. Buy yourself a drink like a big girl."

"I left my money in my car. Will you just buy me a drink and I'll pay you back?"

It's a tough call. I believe her, and it's a good excuse to be together outside of the club, but it could just be her playing games. I decide that it's probably better to stick to my guns.

"No. Why don't you go tool some guy for a drink and then come back and we'll talk like normal people?"

There's a long pause.

"But I want to tool you."

Hey, in Hollywood that's almost a sweet thing to say. Her voice reveals that she's afraid that I'll walk off again if she leaves my sight. She's right.

"Well, that's too bad. You can go get a drink or you can stay here and talk with the most interesting guy you'll ever meet. Besides, I don't like it when girls drink, so I'd rather you didn't."

"Ok."

We walk to part of the bar that's closed down and sit in patio chairs as we talk about our travels. She's more well traveled than I, but my enthusiasm for the places I've been levels the playing field.

At one point we get up and dance. I'm an awful dancer, but I'll admit that the prospect of being that close to her is seductive.

Katya joins us, making me the unlikely hero of the club since I'm now dancing with the two most attractive girls in it.

Finally closing time arrives and we walk back to the main bar where we first met. I turn to my friends to make arrangements to eat, and Dara gets immediately swarmed by a mob of identical lame guys holding business cards.

I glance over and she looks as if she's being accosted by the paparazzi.

"Do you want my business card?"

"Will you call me?"

I hear the idiots begging for her attention and I smile. I know that she's only thinking about one guy. We're ready to leave, so I cut past the mob of guys in black suits and say, "Hey, I'm out of here. I had fun talking to you and I'm sorry we'll never see each other again."

One half turn towards the door.

"WAIT! We have to see each other again."

"Well, we met up this time by accident, maybe it will happen again."

"Don't you want my number?"

"Honestly, yes. But I won't call you because I met you at a club. It doesn't make sense, but it's how I am."

I've caught her off guard.

She laughs and says, "I'm totally like that too! But not with you. We're different! Give me your number and I'll call you."

The army of lame guys have stopped pushing their cards on her and have started to watch the spectacle I'm creating. Shock is visible on their faces, unable to comprehend how I have her so interested in me.

"I would, but you're drunk and you'll forget."

I know she's not drunk.

"No I'm not! I'll totally call you, I promise!"

"Ok, fine."

She gets a pen and paper from one of her impromptu suitors. I love the irony.

"It's 213-555...."

I allow myself to be distracted by my friends' conversation.

Desperate now, she yells, "Hey! Give me your number!"

"I already did!"

"No you didn't. You only gave me the first few numbers."

I slowly give her the number from the beginning. The sea of men swarm her again, interrupted only for a moment as I give her a peck on the lips. I'm acting as if this is an everyday occurrence because I want her to realize that I'm in her league.

Inside I'm bursting with excitement, which I share with everyone in the car.

Tyler is impressed but warns me that she may not call. I'm fully aware of this as only one week prior I stole a girl from Jeremy Piven. She begged for my number in a similar way but never called.

Only after I called three times did she finally answer and agree to meet up.

Hollywood is strange when it comes to phones.

I go back to the house, thrilled with my success. It's the best job I've done to date. I sit with Style in his staircase and excitedly tell him about what happened.

In the middle of my story my phone shows that I've gotten a voicemail. I check it over the speakerphone and we listen, "Hey, Herbal! It's me, Dara! I TOLD you that I'd call you! I'm for real! Call me."

She left her number twice to make sure that I didn't miss it. I searched for her name on Google and found out that she even had model trading cards which people traded for $5 on *eBay*!

Ultimately we talked on the phone several times, but never saw each other again. I started dating Katya the next week so I put her to the side.

As you read my report you should have been able to understand why I said and did everything. If that wasn't the case, re-read the book and try again. The motives behind each one of my statements and actions should be clearly understood.

The 100% Perfect Girl Story

The 100% perfect girl is originally from a Japanese book of short stories. Style found it and adapted it for use as a story to tell girls.

When he originally taught it to me I wasn't paying enough attention so I didn't hear it all. I filled in the blanks myself and tried it out.

I found that the story caused girls to realize that they would only have one opportunity to get to know me, which in turn made them much more eager to exchange numbers at the end of the night.

There's usually no convenient way to transition to this story, so feel free to just announce that you're going to tell her a story.

Once upon a time in Austin, Texas (change this to the city you live in), there was a boy.

One day he left his apartment to do his laundry. He headed down 5th street, going East.

At the same time, there was a beautiful girl who had to mail a package. She left her apartment and just happened to be going West down 5th street.

As luck would have it, they were walking on the same side of the road.

After a while they came within view of each other. Each noticed the other one, as people often do.

As they drew closer, they both had this strange feeling that there might be something special about the other one.

It turns out that they were right. He was the 100% perfect boy for her. He was compatible in every way possible, as if he was born for her. She was also the 100% perfect girl for him in every way. The chances of having two people meet who are actually 100% perfect for each other are almost zero, but it's these special situations that stories are written about.

Soon they were twenty feet away, then ten, then five, then two, then one.

As they passed both felt a surge of emotions in their stomachs, as if they were riding a roller coaster. After passing her he felt as though he'd done something wrong.

He stopped in his tracks and looked back.

She had also stopped, and when their eyes met they laughed.

A conversation was struck. It was awkward at first, but before long they spoke as if they'd been friends all their lives.

An incredible connection was created.

Before they knew it, hours had passed and it began to get dark. Doubt crossed their minds.

"I feel weird just meeting you on the street like this. It's not normal."

She nodded in sad agreement

."Here," she began, "let's go our separate ways. If it is meant to be, then fate will put us together again and we will get married that day!" He reluctantly agreed and they traced their paths back to their homes.

The next day each of them was sure that they would meet that day.

She spent extra time doing her makeup and hair. He put on his best clothes. Each made appointments and ran errands all day, giving fate every opportunity to cross their paths.

But they didn't see each other.

The rest of the week followed in a similar manner, but they didn't meet. A month passed. After a year passed, they rarely thought of each other anymore.

Before they knew it they had each given up hope and over the years they dated other people who were 25%, 50%, or maybe even as high as 72% perfect for them, but never that perfect match that they could have had.

Both of them got married eventually, had children, and completely forgot about the other.

Many years passed, and their respective spouses died. One year a particularly hard flu went around and he caught it. He was in the hospital recovering one day when he decided to go for a walk. He left his room and pushed his IV down the hallway as he walked to the East. Just then he saw a woman approaching from the West.

It was the girl he had met so many years before, but he didn't recognize her. They again came closer and closer, just as they had that one day, and each felt a stirring in their chest but couldn't understand why.

Again they passed, but this time they didn't look back. It was the last time they ever saw one another.

When you finish the story, take a minute and pause. Usually she will say that it's a sad story.

Use this opportunity to say something to the effect of, "Well, I don't think it's a sad story. It just means that fate gives you amazing opportunities and you have to take advantage of them.

"Once fate gives you what you want, you can't just push it away and assume you'll get it again. That's like winning the lottery and ripping the ticket because you can just win again."

If the mood has now gotten too heavy, try talking about other crazy coincidences that made a big difference in your life. I love the story, and I've seen girls months after I stopped calling them who have told me that they still remember the story I told them.

The Cube Routine

Ahh, the cube. The one magical routine that has never failed to interest a girl. It can be done within the first few minutes of talking to her to hook her, or later on to build a connection with her.

The cube is another fabulous routine brought into popularity by Style. It was actually a psychology experiment on which a book was written, but Style adapted it.

Tell her that you're going to ask her five questions and will be able to know everything about her personality.

"Do you ever do those personality quizzes in Cosmo? I used to steal my girlfriend's Cosmos and take the quizzes, but they were always stupid and never accurate. There's actually one quiz, though, that's totally accurate. It was invented by a psychologist and I can do it on you. It's only five questions, and I'll know everything there is to know about your personality."

Giving her plenty of time to answer, ask her to imagine that she's in a big empty desert.

In order, tell her to imagine the following objects in the desert in detail :

A cube (How big is it? Is it on the ground or in the air? What is it made out of?)

A ladder (How close is it to the cube? How tall is it? Is it
    sturdy enough to climb?)
Flowers (How close are they to the cube? How do they
    make you feel? What are they like?)
A horse (Is he moving towards the cube or away? What's
    his personality like?)
A storm (How bad is it? Is it moving towards or away
    from the cube?)

Allow her to give as much detail as she's willing to
give. The more you have the better of an experience you
can make it for her.

Tell her that each of the items represents a part of her
life, as she probably guessed.

Interpreting her results is up to you. If you can make
educated guesses based on stories she's told you, feel free
to take them into account.

Here are some general guidelines that seem to be
true:

For the cube, the size of it corresponds with her self
image. Large is really confident, medium is a healthy self
image, and small is shy and sometimes insecure.

If the cube is in the air she's a dreamer, if it's on the
ground she's grounded and practical.

The material corresponds with her personality - use
your imagination here. Ice means that she's hard to get to
know. Warm means that she's warm and friendly. Glass
means that she doesn't hide secrets.

The ladder represents her goals in life. The closer to
the cube it is, the more focused on her goals she is right
now. If it's tall she has lofty ambitions, if it's short she
doesn't need much to be happy, or she's close to her goals.

Whether or not it's sturdy corresponds with how
confident she is in acheiving her goals.

Flowers represent her friends. If they're close to
the cube, she has really close friends. If they're further
away, most of her friends are more like acquaintances. If

they're one color she tends to like the same type of person, if they're different she's friends with a wide variety of people.

The horse represents her ideal lover. The things she says about his personality are what she looks for in a guy (pay attention!). If it's moving towards the cube say that she wants a new love interest, if it's moving away, then she's getting over someone or moving apart from a current love interest. If it's standing still then either her relationship is stagnating or there isn't a significant love interest in her life.

Whatever you do, don't tell her anything that would indicate that someone she's dating now is the right one for her.

The storm represents problems in her life. If it's large she has some big issues she's working with. If it's small she's carefree. If it's moving towards her there are problems she's stressed about that she knows she'll have to tackle soon. Moving away means that she's finishing dealing with something tough.

Speak with absolute confidence. She doesn't expect you to get them all right, but if you speak with confidence she will look for you to be correct and be willing to stretch things a bit.

Honestly I have been surprised at how accurate the cube is. It's a lot of fun for her, and also for me.

While she's answering the questions initially, occasionally say things like "Oh REALLY?" or, "Hmm... I would have expected that." Comments such as these help build up the suspense and make it a more fun game for her.

Practice the cube on your friends and family first to gain confidence. Within a few tries you won't need to write anything down and you'll remember all of the items in the desert.

At the very end, ask her how accurate it is on a scale from 1–10. I always do this, and the average is probably around 8.5.

Not bad.

Openers

Here are some consistent openers that I've used effectively. Try them out and find one that works for you. As you become more confident and skilled, try switching to just introducing yourself and telling the girl you want to meet her.

Most of these are made up by other pickup artists and I've tried to give proper credit where due. I've chosen openers with a high success rate that are not commonly used.

Dating for Dummies

I heard of someone doing this one many years ago when I first started pickup and I adapted it to be a little more polished. I think Twentysix might be the originator.

Go to a book store and get "Dating for Dummies". It's bright yellow and black—very conspicuous.

Flip to the page that says "NEVER USE THESE LINES", which I think is page 78.

Walk up to a girl, hold the book up in front of your face so that she can see the title, and slowly lower it. Read the first line in a mock nervous voice.

"Hey. do you... uhh... come here often...?"

She'll laugh and answer. Read the next one.

"Hey, baby. What's your sign?"

She'll laugh again.

"Oh my god. This really works! Here, try it!"

Usually she'll keep playing along at this point. On one page there's a hilarious overview of the different types of hugs. Find that page and try some out. The "tent hug" is particularly comical.

If she refuses to play along, find the section on breaking up.

"Ok, you're forcing me to do this. One second... Umm... Our time together has been magical and you have made me a better man. However, I feel as though we are drifting apart and no longer share the same values. I like you as a person, but feel that it would be best for both of us if we were just friends... also I cheated on you twice."

Thug Name

This one was made up by Jlaix from Real Social Dynamics.

"Hey guys, I'm thinking about becoming a thug and hardcore gangsta rapper. What do you think is a better thug name: 'Deacon Fresh D-Lite' or 'Extra Sauce Murder Killa'? I feel like both of them really fit my personality."

After you determine your thug name, make up names for them too like "Devious Honey G Sweetness".

Sugar Momma

Walk up to a group of two or three girls.

"Hey, which one of you guys is the richest? I'm sick of working and I'm ready to get a sugar momma."

After they work it out,

"Ok, cool. So we'll go get married in a few minutes. First, we need someone to cook for us, though... which one of you is the best chef?"

Printed in Great Britain
by Amazon.co.uk, Ltd.,
Marston Gate.